GW01466387

TE~

Tri~~ SCIENCE

# The Human Body

John Stringer

Published by
Hopscotch Educational Publishing Ltd,
29 Waterloo Place,
Leamington Spa CV32 5LA
Tel: 01926 744227

© 2001 Hopscotch Educational Publishing

Written by John Stringer
Series design by Blade Communications
Illustrated by Bernard Connors
Printed by Clintplan, Southam

ISBN 1-902239-68-7

# Contents

# About the series

**Teaching the Tricky Bits** arose out of a frustrated teacher's cry for help when one of the children in her class said 'But why do we need blood?' She sort-of knew the answer but couldn't quite explain it so that the child could understand.

And so began the development of a series of books designed to inform non-specialist teachers about the different science topics in the National Curriculum.

But soon we realised that often information on science tends to be dry and can only be taken in in bite-sized pieces for fear of falling asleep. So we agreed that we needed a series of books that would keep teachers informed and awake!

This is what we have achieved. This book, and the other three in the series, all contain vital, useful and fascinating information written by John Stringer, who is adviser to the Channel 4 series 'Fourways Farm' and 'Making Sense of Science', and writer of many primary science resources.

But just as important as the information John has supplied is the approach he has taken with his writing – it's fun to read! There are amusing scenarios and anecdotes. You really won't fall asleep!

Then we realised that it's all well and good having all this information and rolling about in the aisles laughing, but what are you going to do with it? Or, more importantly, what are the children going to do with your new-found knowledge?

So, John has provided relevant activities for each chapter, starting with what could be done at level 1 and going all the way to level 5.

This makes these books ideal for every teacher. You can allocate activities according to ability. You can still use the book if you find yourself teaching a different age group.

We hope you enjoy reading and using this book as much as we have enjoyed putting it together!

**Other titles in the series are:**

## Forces, electricity and magnetism
### (and the Earth in space)

ISBN 1 902239 69 5

## Materials

ISBN 1 902239 70 9

## Plants and animals

ISBN 1 902239 71 7

# Introduction

This is a different sort of science book. In eight chapters, it aims to give you a better understanding of one of the areas of science that teachers find tricky – the human body. It does this in three ways.

- First of all, each of the chapters contains some easy-to-read text about your body – what it does and how it works.

- Second, each chapter has some novel activities that will help you – and your children – learn more about how the body works, and practise the skills of science.

- Third, there are 'fascinating facts' throughout. These are amazing bits of information that your children will want to learn and swap with their friends.

No book this length can cover the extraordinary complexity of our bodies. Some areas are not addressed, where they are not appropriate to the primary school curriculum. So, you will not find much on glands and hormones, for example. But the basic body systems are all here – described and explained in everyday language.

Our bodies are an everyday miracle. This book will help you and your children to recognise that miracle – and to value it.

## So, how do we know we're alive?

### The seven signs of life

It may seem perfectly obvious to you which things around us are alive, and which things are not. Your dog moves and is alive; your car moves but is not. The television is motionless and is not alive; the spider plant is motionless but is alive. This may not be so obvious to children. We take it for granted that we are alive. We demonstrate (most of us!) the seven essential life processes:

### 1 We take in and use food for energy

– sometimes more than is good for us. Some of this food is used for growth – wanted and unwanted – and some for repair and maintenance. (See Chapter 1.)

### Fascinating facts

- Your body is made of 65 per cent water. An adult male has the equivalent of eight wellington boots full of water in his body.

- There are between fifty and seventy-five trillion cells in the human body. Stomach cells live for two days; bone cells for 25–30 years; brain cells for your whole lifetime.

- Snorers can reach a sound level of 65 or more decibels, compared with 70–90 for a pneumatic drill.

### 2 We move

– animals move while plants appear not to. Plants do move, of course, but very slowly. Animals have to move, since they don't make their own food. Green plants can afford to be lazy – they make their own food, sitting around and using the sunlight to produce food by photosynthesis. Lacking this talent, animals have to move around and look for food – sometimes plants, sometimes each other. Animals that don't move from one place to another have to make the most of passing opportunities. Sea anemones grab passing plankton, and barnacles were once described as 'lying on their backs and kicking their food into their mouths'. (See Chapter 2.)

### 3 We grow

– we don't expand like a balloon; we add material to our bodies. This process never stops. It's not just that we grow as children; we keep adding material to our bodies to repair damage and wear and tear. Someone has calculated that if our skin were made from stainless steel, it would last us about seven years. Since it is constantly being renewed, it lasts us a lifetime – albeit with more sag and less elasticity as we get older. The lost bits drop off and form the majority of the house dust that accumulates in corners and crevices. This provides a useful food for bed mites and other minute living things. But let's not think about that!

You are growing, repairing and renewing all the time. Most living things start off small and get bigger. Children are fascinated by the really big – dinosaurs, tall trees and whales. But these are small fry compared with the largest fungi, which may be kilometres across – even if their bodies are simply tangles of underground tissue. In fact, the biggest fungus is underground in the USA and is 600ha (1,500 acres in area).

Things grow by adding to themselves. This contrasts with balloons and umbrellas, which grow by stretching. You can understand children getting the two confused. Most growing plants and animals do not 'swell up' – and indeed many plants become more complex as they grow, adding more roots and branches. (Animals do not, as a rule, add more legs or heads to their bodies, although they may need more scales, feathers or hair.) There are exceptions to the 'swelling' rule, but they are mostly microscopic.

## 4 We can reproduce

– some of us choose not to, and others, sadly, find it difficult, but the majority of humans can and do reproduce. This is just as well, since we all have a fleeting lifespan and our young will take our places – like it or not – in due course. Until we find the key to eternal life, any species that fails to reproduce is doomed to extinction.

Life is finite, and if living things did not reproduce, then life would quickly die out on Earth. Virtually all living things reproduce – though where they are sterile, as in the case of worker ants, they have an important role to play in the reproduction of their colony or society. (See Chapter 3.)

## 5 We respire

– this isn't just breathing. In fact, that's just the start of the story, but breathing is the bit we recognise and the sign we commonly take that life is still possible, whatever other signs an immobile body may lack. The true process of respiration is using food to release energy – a process very similar to burning. It takes place in all our cells. (See Chapter 4.)

## 6 We respond to stimuli

– that is, we are aware of what is going on around us and respond accordingly. From the unconscious responses (our pupils growing larger as we walk into the darkened cinema) to the conscious (carefully checking our lottery numbers as they turn up on the screen or are read to us by the announcer), we react to the multiple stimuli that we receive from the world around us. It is said that babies are born into a 'booming, buzzing confusion' – and maybe the first and toughest job we have to learn is how to filter out the stimuli we can live without.

We have confused the issue, of course, by making things that mimic sensitivity. Burglar alarms that respond to movement, switches that react to human proximity and greenhouse vents that open on hot days are among them. But these hardly compare with animal and human sensitivity. Dogs can detect and distinguish thousands of smells, mating butterflies can locate each other from miles away and we can identify a huge range of colours.

Human sensitivity is mostly through the five familiar senses. (See Chapter 5.)

## 7 Finally, we produce waste

– some of it is gaseous – carbon dioxide from our lungs, less pleasant gases from other places – and some is liquid and solid waste. Excretion is the general name for all these waste-ridding activities and is common to everything that lives.

## Fascinating facts

- The noise you hear when you listen to a heart beat is the sound of the heart valves slapping shut. Your heart is in the middle of your chest; but the bottom tip touches the chest wall, on your left.

# So what's alive and what's not?

### Is fire alive?

Perhaps the most difficult phenomenon to define as non-living is fire. Fire needs to feed, it moves and grows, it can produce other fires, it uses oxygen to consume, it responds to wind, to rain and to fire-fighters' hoses and it leaves behind it its own waste products. No wonder children have trouble with agreeing that it is non-living when they compare it with a tree.

### Is a tree alive?

Trees discretely manufacture their own food, they totally fail to walk, stretch or play league badminton, they grow so slowly that we fail to notice the changes, they may carry green flowers that are scarcely noticeable, they respire without breathing (exchanging gases through modest pores in their leaves), they have a response rate to stimuli measurable in years rather than milliseconds and their waste products, demurely encased in red and brown leaves, are so much a part of autumn that we hardly notice them.

### Is an apple that has been picked alive?

Before you start getting too know-all about all of this, consider whether you know a living thing when you see one. Treat yourself. Have an apple.

Now, is that apple alive or dead? You'd say 'Dead, of course – except for the seeds,' wouldn't you? The seeds could live – become an apple tree, have little Cox's orange pippins of their own. So they have the potential for life. Fair enough. But is the apple alive?

Not if it's rotting. Life has now ceased for that apple, and the natural processes of decay, helped along by other living things like bacteria and fungi, are reducing that apple to a nasty brown puddle. But what if the apple is fresh? Is it alive?

If not, then when did it die? Did it give a ghastly death rattle as you snapped it from the tree? No? Did it die later of wounds or shock? No? Then it must still be alive, mustn't it? In fact, it is still respiring – taking in oxygen to support its life processes and giving out carbon dioxide. And it is still responding to stimuli. It may ripen nicely after picking – especially if it is kept in the light.

## Fascinating facts

- When your tummy rumbles, you can hear gas bubbling through your guts. The gas is made by gut bacteria, digesting your food. Bacteria get more to digest from beans and other vegetables, so these foods make more gas.

- The noise you hear when you put a seashell to your ear sounds like the sea, but it is the blood swishing through the blood vessels of your ear flap.

- Squishing sounds from your tummy are from food being pushed through your gut, like toothpaste along a tube.

No wonder children have difficulty with the concept of living and non-living. So do we.

And how about Pharaoh's corn? Seeds from ancient Egypt, thousands of years old, have been taken from the tombs of the Pharaohs and germinated to produce new plants. Was that corn alive as a seed or not? The answer is that it was alive, but only just. It needs the right conditions to germinate. Any other answer means that life is newly created every time these seeds germinate.

So – there's bad news for vegetarians and fruit-bats. We eat fresh fruit and vegetables alive!

# Why do I have to eat?

## My body bag

**Many young children think that their body is a kind of skin bag that holds all food, blood and waste. Stomachs are commonly imagined to be large, low-slung containers, and they may have two exits, corresponding with the double functions of lavatories. But some children may have connected the stomach with the breaking down of food and possibly sense that it is transferred somewhere else in the body.**

### What do you know about food?

This depends on what you read last. First you hear that red wine is good for you, then it is bad for you; milk is a complete food, milk is fattening; all fats are harmful, some fats are essential to body functions. Advice changes day by day, making teaching about balanced diet very difficult at any time.

We need a range of foods for healthy living. These can be provided from a variety of sources, and commonly include carbohydrates for energy, fats for both energy and general body functions, proteins for growth and repair, and small amounts of vitamins and minerals for general health and resistance to disease. Water is also essential for life. We can obtain these foods from many different sources, including plants and animals – a balanced diet provides them in the right quantities.

The word 'diet', however, is almost always associated with weight loss – and not with the balanced intake of foods that should characterise healthy eating. Similarly, the main food groups may be known by name, but children have preconceptions about them which you need to address. They need a clear understanding of key words: fitness, health, diet, exercise; and food groups: fats (butter, milk, cheese, plant oils), proteins (meat, fish, eggs, some pulses), carbohydrates (bread, cereals, pasta, rice, couscous), vitamins (fruit, vegetables, seeds), minerals (most foods) and fibre or roughage (mostly the cellulose – a carbohydrate – found in plant walls, such as in cereals, fruit and vegetables).

Sugar gives us energy, but has no other nutrient value. It is an important part of our diet, but it is hard to control intake when we eat it without knowing. Go on a sugar search, looking at the labels on packaged and tinned foods. While many foods have a recognisable sugar content, it can crop up in some surprising places – among them: baked beans, barbecue sauce and instant soups. Try a salt search, too. Most people eat twice their needs and for some of them this can raise blood pressure. You might be surprised at the more unusual uses of sugar or salt. For example, you may find sugar in tomato sauce, and salt in 'healthy' cereal bars.

### Our children need our help

Children's heights and weights vary across a wide range. Not everyone can, or should, be a supermodel. An excessively fatty diet leads to the build-up of fat globules in the blood. There are many 'good' diets and some are chosen for sound cultural or medical reasons.

## Fascinating facts

- Your stomach will reject anything more than it can handle – or anything that irritates the stomach lining. If you stretch your stomach too far, it will tell your brain that it is in pain. This is stomach-ache. The vomit centre in the brain gets signals from your body – which include the signals it sends when you are standing at the back of a cross-channel ferry. If the signals are strong enough, they trigger a convulsion of your stomach muscles, and you are sick. The sour taste is from the acids working in your stomach.

We are all unique and our lifestyles vary. A balanced diet and regular exercise are essential for health. There are few intrinsically good or bad foods or means of exercise – we all need to develop a lifestyle that suits our individual needs.

There have been many surveys on our children's health over the years. Some have presented disturbing evidence of a high intake of fatty foods and little exercise, with a half of girls, and a third of boys, not even exercising for the equivalent of a brisk ten minute walk each week.

Most of us are aware of the major food groups and the importance and characteristics of each. 'Traffic light' and 'star' systems of classifying school meals help to draw the attention of children to the relative nutritional value of different foods. Packaged foods are clearly labelled and ingredients identified. But it is harder to regulate frequency. On average, a third of the population eats or drinks something every hour between seven in the morning and midnight. Food habits are formed before school, and for primary children these are likely to reflect family values and parental choice as well as their own decisions. In these circumstances, simply recording the content of different foods is not enough to change children's eating patterns, but you can help with the process of health education.

## Why do we need exercise?

Reasons may include the need to exercise the heart and to fill the lungs (aerobic exercise), to burn off excess fat and to keep muscle and bone systems in condition. Many people experience the benefits of regular exercise. They include greater resistance to illness, especially heart disease and chest infections.

We need exercise – this need not be violent but should be enjoyable and should set a pattern for life.

Indeed, aerobic activities are intended to be sustained for long periods. They can be grouped under strength, stamina and suppleness and most contribute to more than one. But dancing and fencing are especially good for suppleness, rowing and swimming for strength and cycling and brisk walking for stamina.

### Fascinating facts

● During your life, you will eat the equivalent weight of 14 adult elephants (without the tusks). You can expect to eat 80,000 meals, running your gut continuously for 650,000 hours.

## Where does our food go?

### Does someone collect it?

Your food has a lengthy tunnel journey ahead of it. It may be inside your gut for 24 to 48 hours, and be squirted with 17 different chemicals. Your digestive system is the place where food is broken down into a suitable state to go into the bloodstream. It all takes place below the heart and lungs in your tummy or, more correctly, your abdomen. Here, the chewed food is thoroughly munched up with chemicals that help to dissolve it. Your stomach can hold about as much gunge as a large pop bottle – around two litres. It takes about two to four hours to turn your meal into a thick soup that is squirted into your small intestine. The first part of this journey is through a 30cm length of small intestine called the duodenum, where digestive juices – enzymes from the pancreas and bile from the liver – are added. The bile squirts in like washing-up liquid.

Through the rest of the 6.5m of the 2.5cm-wide small intestine, the food is absorbed into the bloodstream ready for your body to use. The velvety lining of the small intestine acts like blotting paper, soaking up all the useful materials and passing a thick pasty sludge into the large intestine.

The shorter (1.8m), wider (7.5cm) large intestine is full of harmless bacteria that help break down the rest of the food so that the body can use the water and minerals. The remaining food waste – coloured brown by pigments from the bile – begins to pile up behind the anus, waiting for you to go to the lavatory.

Your food is pushed along on its journey by waves of muscular squeezes. These work so well that you can eat and swallow when you are upside down – or in weightless conditions in space.

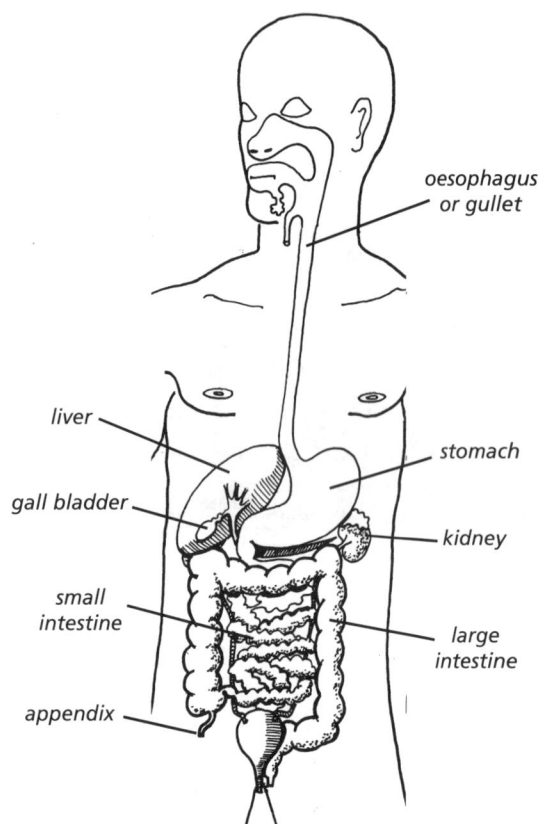

oesophagus
or gullet

liver

gall bladder

small
intestine

appendix

stomach

kidney

large
intestine

## Fascinating facts

- Fibre is hardly digested at all. It fills your large intestine, pushing out food that has dried out and is hard to get rid of. Fibre-rich foods, like brown rice and wholemeal bread, help deal with constipation.

## Fascinating facts

- Each American produces about ten bins of wasted food every year.

- Your stomach stops digesting if you are very frightened, preparing your body for danger. You get butterflies or cramps.

- Diarrhoea or runny tummy is a safety mechanism set off by food that irritates. Your gut pushes all its contents through in a rush, to prevent damage.

- Earthworms can make a good, crunchy snack.

Micro-organisms have both a damaging and a beneficial role. If all the world's micro-organisms were eliminated, the world would come to a speedy standstill. Humans, unable to digest their food, would die up to their necks in waste because micro-organisms are essential to many of our body processes and live both in and on us in huge numbers. A really hot chicken tikka will wipe out many of the bacteria in our intestines, replacing them with fresh, more curry-tolerant intestinal flora.

Bacteria and other micro-organisms break down every form of human waste, returning it to the cycle without which life would end. Some are harmful, of course, and they cause disease and infection. But most are beneficial to us in many ways.

## Get your teeth into this

### How many? – A mouthful!

If you take care of them, you should have the full adult set of 32 teeth. These are the hardest objects in the whole body, because on the outside is a thin layer of extremely hard enamel which covers the hard dentine coat. But teeth are alive – as we all know when we get toothache – with their own blood supply and nerves, running into the soft pulp cavity.

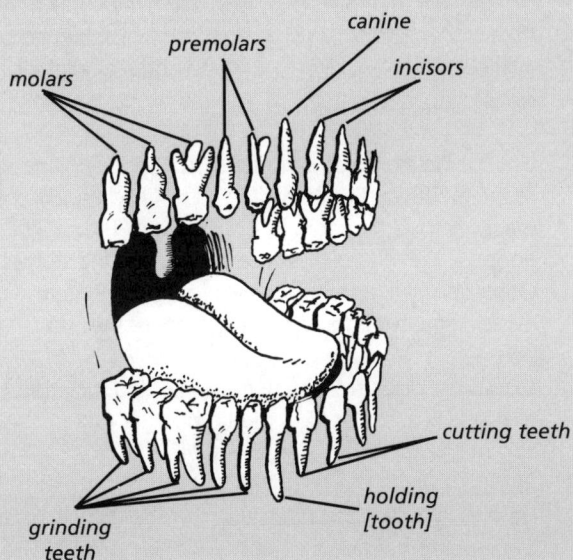

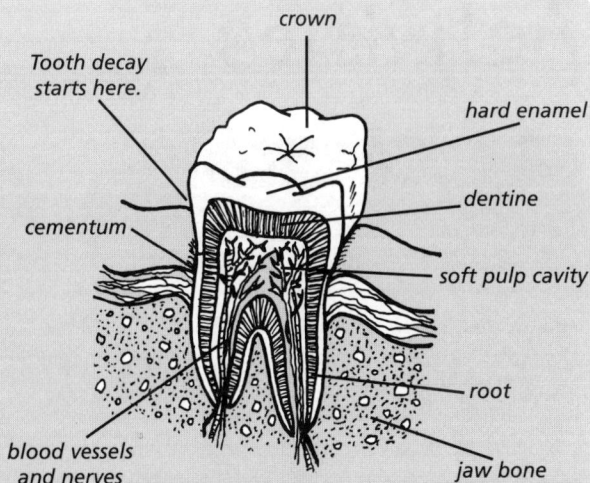

crown

Tooth decay starts here.

hard enamel

dentine

cementum

soft pulp cavity

root

blood vessels and nerves

jaw bone

molars

premolars

canine

incisors

cutting teeth

holding [tooth]

grinding teeth

### All the better to eat you with!

Cutting incisors, gripping canines and grinding premolars and molars all combine to break down your food, while spit or saliva is mixed with it to soften it and make it easier to swallow. Saliva has an enzyme in it that breaks down food. A dry cream cracker will become sweet and sugary if you chew it for long enough, but you can't swallow more than two without a drink, because the saliva isn't enough to wash the dry biscuit down.

### Clean your teeth!

To slow the formation of plaque which causes tooth decay and gum disease we should clean teeth and gums regularly, especially using a fluoride toothpaste. We should visit the dentist twice a year for an inspection and avoid eating sweets except immediately after meals and just before cleaning our teeth.

A school health visitor once said that many of the families she worked with had no toothbrush, or had a shared brush. Also, notice that most toothbrush ads are in the summer, when tourists replace their brushes in case the hotel maid sees the old one!

Chewed fibrous sticks were used by our ancestors to clean their teeth and are still in use in many parts of the world. They contain natural anti-bacterial agents, and are both hygienic and biodegradable – you chew one, use it and throw it away.

## Fascinating facts

- Babies' jaws are too small to hold the whole adult complement of 32 teeth, so children have 20 milk teeth at first, which are gradually replaced by the 32 adult teeth later.

- Crunching on hard sweets in the dark can produce sparks.

# Activities

## Level One

Talk to the children about why we have to eat. Explain why we eat in terms of activity, health, growth and repair.

Ask the children to tell you about their diets. Let them draw and label pictures of favourite meals. Are there foods in them that will give them energy for activity, and material for health, growth and repair?

Broadly classify familiar foods into 'foods for growth' and 'foods for energy'.

## Level Two

Ask the children to record their diets over a short period and to look at how healthy they are. Ask them to suggest how they might make them 'healthier' diets.

Compare their food diaries with a model diet. Discuss ways that they could improve their diets, but avoid the idea that all the 'nice' foods have to be cut out. Suggest that an intake of all foods in moderation is important.

Remember that young children have little choice over many of the foods they eat – their main meals, for example. Investigate the meals served in school, the contents of a specially prepared lunch box, or the snacks that the school has in the tuck shop.

## Level Three

Investigate teeth. Help the children to learn the names and functions of different teeth. Ask them to make 'mouth maps' of their teeth (including missing teeth, fillings and other differences). Devise some rules that will help to ensure dental health. Find out about milk teeth and adult teeth.

Find out more about tooth care from a health professional. Make a tooth care plan and see who can stick to it for a week, recording what they do on a chart.

## Level Four

Categorise the foods the children eat as providers of carbohydrates, proteins, fats, vitamins and mineral salts. Ask the children to record their intake of each and state how balanced they think their diet is. Where are there deficiencies? Where are there excesses? How could their diet be improved?

Devise a balanced diet that contains the main food groups. Compare that with the diet the children regularly eat. Suggest some ways that their choices of school meal would improve their diet.

## Level Five

Ask the children to research and explain the functions of the main organs of the digestive system. Each child could take one organ and then the group could pool their research to give an idea of how the whole gut works.

Use the classroom as a model of the gut, using one door as the mouth and the other the anus. Children take their places around the room as body organs. They might carry hoops – 'Crawl through the hoop to enter the stomach.' Other children make their way through the system, explaining what is happening to them as they go.

Model the digestive system from recycled materials, using a large box as the trunk, a plastic bottle for the stomach and plastic tube for the gut.

Help the children to understand that the food they eat is to power respiration that takes place in the cells. They should be able to explain why each cell needs energy, and how it reaches the cells.

Link the children's understanding of our need for food and the removal of waste products with the need for gas exchange (Chapter 4) and the way the blood system works (Chapter 6).

# How do I move?

**Animals are unable to make their own food and because of that, they have had to develop ways of moving to food sources.**

Once a living thing moves, it needs sense organs to find its way around. Putting the sense organs at the front or top of the body makes them more useful. If the animal is a secondary consumer – a predator or carnivore – the sense organs are likely to be forward-facing, enabling it to see its prey and to catch it efficiently. If the animal is a primary consumer or herbivore, then its sense organs are likely to survey the surroundings more generally, because it needs to be aware of predators and danger. Cats have eyes on the front of their heads while mice have them on the side. Cats have excellent, stereoscopic forward vision to catch mice and mice have good all-round vision to spot and avoid cats. Our forward-facing eyes may not be the result of predatory tendencies. It is likely that they are a useful hangover from the days when we lived in trees and needed to judge the distance to the next branch before jumping.

## The skeleton

Vertebrate animals like us are able to move because they have a jointed internal skeleton made up of bones, with muscles to move them.

The skeleton has a framework of about 200 bones and 100 joints. There are 26 in the backbone, and seven in the neck.

### The skeleton:

- gives the body shape
- protects the inside parts of the body – the ribs protect the heart and lungs and the skull protects the brain.

Our skeleton is made from cartilage or bone or from a combination of these two connective tissues. Humans have a skeleton which comprises a skull, spinal column, ribs, the pelvic and pectoral girdles and the arms and legs.

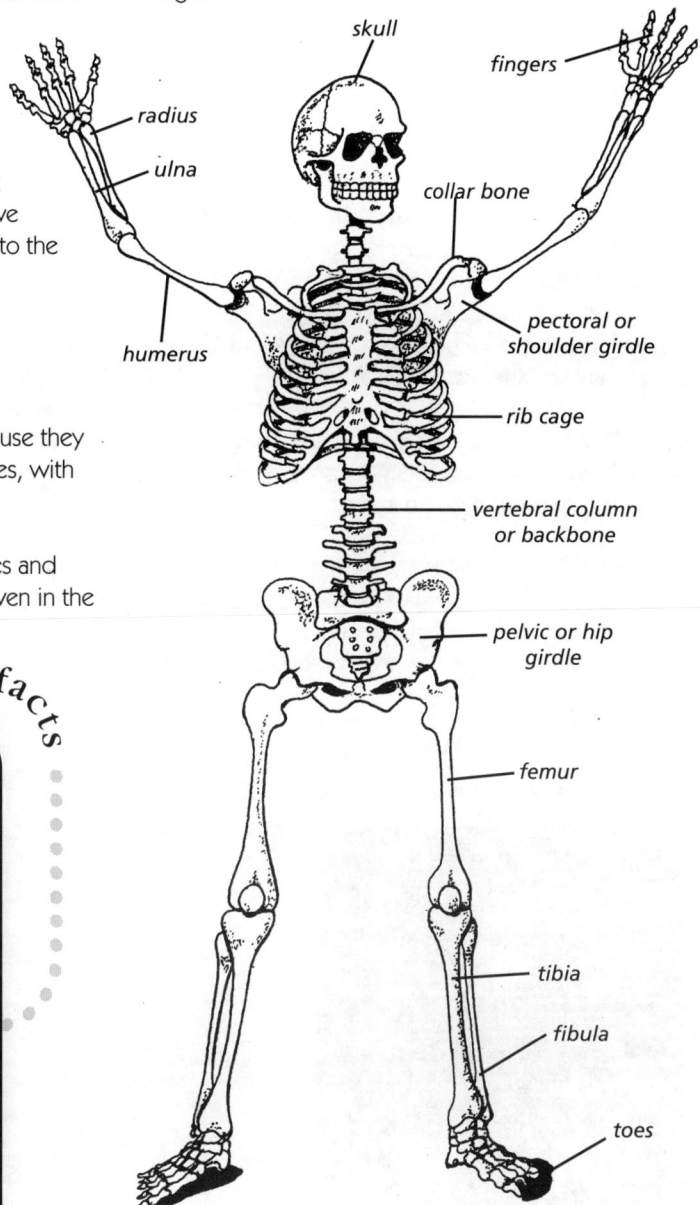

skull

fingers

radius

ulna

collar bone

humerus

pectoral or shoulder girdle

rib cage

vertebral column or backbone

pelvic or hip girdle

femur

tibia

fibula

toes

## Fascinating facts

- Babies are born with between 300 and 350 bones, but some of these fuse together as they grow, so that the average adult total is 206.

- There are 22 skull bones, 26 vertebrae and 60 bones in a pair of arms and hands.

- The collar bone is the commonest bone to break. It is easily broken by a fall onto your hands, which transmit the force through your arms to the collar bone.

## Joints

There are three types of joints between bones:

- The shoulder and hip joints are ball and socket, allowing circular movement.

- The elbow and knee joints are hinge joints, working like a door.

- The wrist and ankle joints are slipping joints, working by rocking slightly.

## Bones

As children grow, the cartilage in their bones is replaced with harder bone. In humans, the process of bone hardening, or ossification, is completed at about the age of 25. The last bone to ossify is the breastbone. Our total number of bones varies with our age; many bones fuse together during the ossification process. The average number of distinct bones in a young human is around 200, not counting the six bony ossicles found in the ears.

### So what is bone?

Bone is the hard material that makes up almost all the adult skeleton. It can be dense or spongy, and it gradually replaces another type of firm skeletal material known as cartilage or gristle. Bone is a mixture of inorganic salts (65 to 70 per cent) and various organic substances (30 to 35 per cent) and is both hard and elastic.

Its hardness comes from its salts like calcium phosphate and calcium carbonate. Its elasticity is from organic substances like gelatine, collagen and fats. Tubes through the bones called Haversian canals contain nerve tissues and blood vessels that provide bones with nourishment. Bone marrow makes up two to five per cent of the body weight of a person. Red bone marrow is the tissue in which red and white blood cells and blood platelets are made.

## Fascinating facts

- Your knuckles crack because pulling on them quickly makes a vacuum in the joints. Fluid rushes into the spaces, making a popping sound.

- Your funny bone is in fact a nerve in your elbow. Knocking it can make your forearm tingle or freeze.

The body is continually replacing bone in response to the stresses and strains of body activity. As you get older, the rate of bone absorption is often faster than that of bone formation, resulting in the condition known as osteoporosis. Symptoms include getting shorter and an increased frequency of fractures.

### Bones break easily

Simple, or closed, fractures are not visible on the surface. Compound, or open, fractures involve a breaking of the skin, often exposing the bone. Single and multiple fractures refer to the number of breaks in the same bone. Fractures are complete if the break is total, or incomplete (greenstick) if the fracture occurs only part of the distance across a bone shaft, sometimes bending or crushing the bone. Incomplete fractures are found mostly in young children, whose bones are more resilient. Heavy impact causes most fractures but the simple activity of throwing a ball could cause a break.

### Why the plaster?

If the broken bits are close, stretching or traction to overcome the pull of powerful muscles may be used to bring them together. If this doesn't work, an operation is usually performed, and the fragments are joined with screws, nuts, bolts, nails, wires or metal plates. Once they are in line, segments are braced with a plaster cast or splint to immobilise the fracture and to speed healing. While healing, the body creates new tissue to join the broken segments. Minerals in the tissue harden to form solid new bone structure.

# Muscles

Muscles are joined to bones, and bones and muscles together enable body movement. Muscles can only pull, not push, which they do by shortening and thickening. So muscles have to work in pairs, pulling in turns to move bones.

Muscles are able to contract, usually in response to a stimulus from the nervous system. This may be a direct order from you – 'I want to stand up!' – or it may be an unconscious order from your brain – 'That food has had long enough sloshing around in the stomach. Move it to the intestine!'

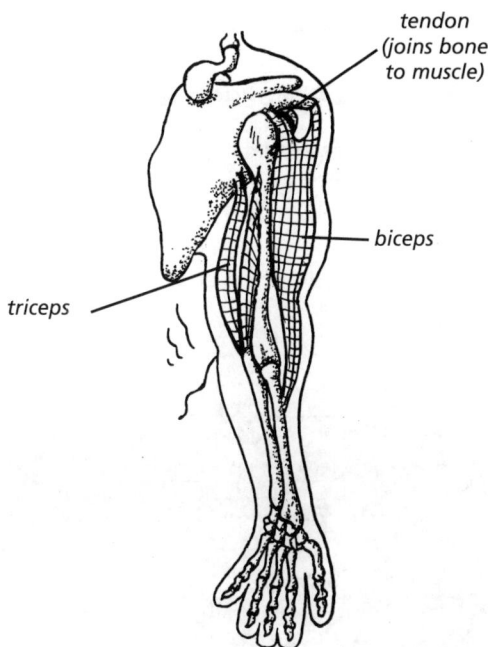

## Skeletal, or striated, muscle

Skeletal or striated muscle is partly under your conscious control. You use it every time you choose to move. But you don't have to think about everyday actions like walking. That's handled for you. This controllable muscle is also called 'voluntary' muscle. Most skeletal muscle is attached to your skeleton by tendons. Contracting skeletal muscles move the various bones and cartilage of your skeleton. Skeletal muscle forms most of the meat that you find at the butcher's.

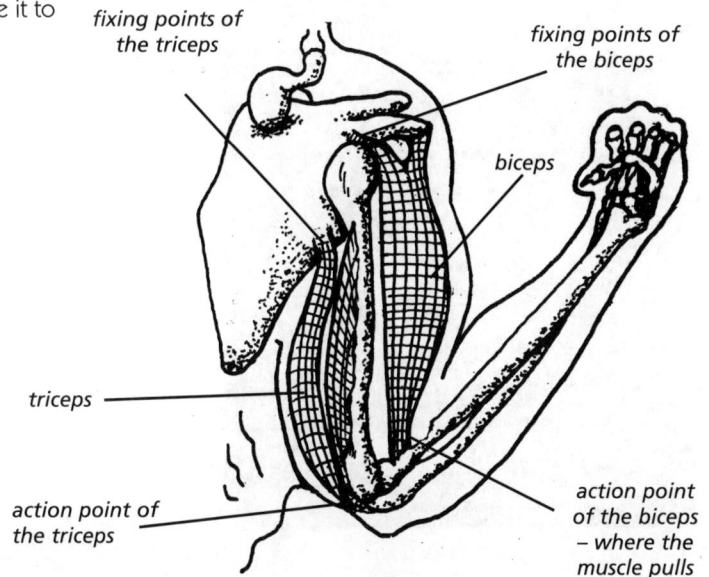

tendon (joins bone to muscle)

biceps

triceps

fixing points of the triceps

fixing points of the biceps

biceps

triceps

action point of the triceps

action point of the biceps – where the muscle pulls

All muscle is made of fibrils, which are minute, threadlike structures composed of complex proteins. The fibrils are made up of alternating rows of thick and thin filaments with their ends interleaved. During muscular contractions, these rows of filaments slide along each other by chemical bridges that act like ratchets, seizing and pulling. But muscles are not all alike. You have three types of muscular tissue: smooth, skeletal or striated, and the special heart muscle – cardiac.

## Smooth muscle

This is the muscle you don't know about. Stimuli for the contractions of smooth muscles are controlled by your unconscious nervous system. You can't instruct them to contract. Smooth muscle is found in your skin, internal organs, reproductive system, major blood vessels and excretory system. So smooth muscles in your bladder relax as they accept the remains of last night's cup of tea. But you need striated muscle to squeeze your bladder when you later decide to go to the loo.

## Cardiac muscle

This muscle tissue makes up most of your heart. It is unique because it works independently, thumping throughout your life. That's why hearts continue to beat during the transplant process. The regular beating of cardiac muscle is not under your control. It is supplied with nerves from the nervous system, but these only speed or slow its action and are not responsible for its continuous beating. You can't help your heart beating faster and you can't tell it to slow down either! (See page 37 for a detailed diagram of the heart.)

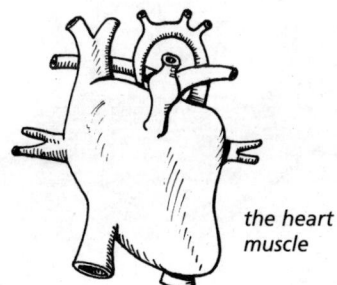

the heart muscle

# Controlling the muscles – the nervous system

The 'wires' of the nervous system are cells called neurones; these can be stimulated to make receiving and transmitting units that can transfer information from one part of the body to another. Each nerve cell has a central portion known as the cell body, and one or more structures referred to as axons and dendrites. The dendrites are short extensions of the cell body, receiving stimuli. They pick up the messages from your touch and pain receptors. The axon is a long wire. It sends the messages from your brain to the other cells. Nerve messages travel very fast – about 400km an hour – but reaction is still not quite instantaneous.

## The body's messengers

Humans have a bony spine and skull for the protection of the central controlling part of the nervous system – the brain and spinal cord. The brain and the spinal cord are linked through an opening in the base of the skull; both are in contact with other parts of the body through the nerves.

## Fascinating facts

- There are between 656 and 850 muscles in your body, depending on which muscles you count as separate. (Some are joined together.)

- Your longest muscle is your sartorius, from your waist to your knee.

- Your largest muscle is the gluteus maximus of your bottom.

- Your muscles can ache during exercise because a waste product called lactic acid builds up in them, causing soreness and stiffness.

- You use 17 muscles to smile and 43 to frown.

- Your jaw muscles can close your chewing teeth with a force of 120 kilograms. (Force is measured in Newtons (N). 120 kilograms is about 1200N or 1.2kN.)

## Exercise matters

Muscles that are given proper exercise react to stimuli quickly and powerfully, and have tone. With exceptional use, muscles may increase in size because of an increase in size of the individual muscle cells. This is body-building. With prolonged disuse, muscles may diminish in size and become weaker. That's what happens if influenza puts you in bed for a week. In some forms of paralysis, the muscles may decline so much that they are reduced to a fraction of their normal size. Use it or lose it!

## Fascinating facts

- You have about 75km of nerves in your body. Messages travel through them at over 120m per second. The nerve is ready for another impulse in less than a hundredth of a second.

- Your sciatic nerve is the thickest and largest in your body. It is the thickness of a pencil and runs from the spinal cord down the back of each leg.

# Activities

### Level One

Ask the children to draw and label their general body shape, to name their limbs and to explain what they use them for. The pictures might include examples of the possible movements, for example 'I can walk and run,' and 'My arms can move like this.'

### Level Two

Explore the bones of the hand. The children could model this using five pipe-cleaners tied together as the basic structure, and then add cut lengths of pipe-cleaner to represent the bones of the fingers and palm. Bend over the pipe-cleaner tips to stop the 'bones' coming off.

Use the constructed hands to model the possible movements of a human hand. Learn about the way the fingers are jointed, and suggest how the muscles might be attached to pull on the bones so that the hand works like this. Try putting a pencil or a hammer in the model hand. How do the fingers work? Why is the opposable thumb – working in the opposite direction to the fingers – so important? (We need it for grip.)

### Level Three

Research, draw and model the skeleton. Simple card models – even those made for Hallowe'en – are quite accurate and can be copied. Make models from card tubes on strings.

Name the main bones. Ask the children to record their function (support, protection or movement). Use reference books to find out more about bones. For example, find out why adults have fewer bones than young children.

### Level Four

Research the muscles of the arms and legs. Measure the amount and strength of movement. How strong are the children's hands? They could measure this by seeing how much a strong spring can be squeezed. How strong are their legs? Put a bathroom scale vertically against the bottom of the wall. Each child lies next to it and presses their foot against the scale. Who can push the hardest? Who has the strongest leg when measured in this way?

### Level Five

Explore and model the ways that bones and muscles interact. Model the bones of the arm using two lengths of stiff card, linked with a paper-fastener. Use elastic bands to model the muscles. How is the lower arm lifted and lowered? Which muscle contracts to do which task? Some construction kits offer strong pieces to articulate; LEGO ® girders can be used, or plastic Meccano. They are stiffer than card, and less likely to collapse. Emphasise that muscles always pull; so to return a bone to its original position, a second muscle will have to pull it back. This is why muscles are paired.

Research the different cells that make up a bundle of muscle fibres. How do they work? How does the contraction occur? Why does it need energy, and what happens to the waste products?

# Where did I come from?

**Children are growing and changing, illustrating the way in which we all change as we mature and age. They may well have had, through family or their pets, experience of both birth and death; they may be beginning to understand the cyclical nature of life.**

While many children can accept that animals reproduce sexually, very few – perhaps because they equate sexual reproduction with copulation – believe that plants reproduce sexually.

Sexual reproduction involves the combining of genetic material from both parents to produce a new individual. It happens with both plants and animals. Sometimes the product of the process doesn't even look alive. Some children believe that hens' eggs and seeds are not alive, though in changed circumstances either may produce new life – though not, of course, 'breakfast eggs' which are not fertilised.

Research has shown that for many children, new life is formed from components or parts – new human babies manufactured 'in a mummy's tummy' from bits, and chicks assembled from kits of legs, wings, head and body floating around inside the egg.

## The human life-cycle

Humans are mammals, which means that instead of squirting a load of eggs into a pond and hoping for the best (fish and amphibians), burying a leathery egg in the sand (reptiles) or laying a great big chalk-covered ovoid (birds), human females retain their young inside themselves until they are ready to be born.

### Fascinating facts

- The heaviest normal new-born child was a boy who weighed 24lb 4oz. He was born on 3 June 1961 to Mrs Saadat Cor of Southern Turkey.

- A premature girl weighing less than ten ounces was born in Tyne and Wear in 1938. She was fed with a fountain-pen filler every hour for the first thirty hours, and survived.

- Elizabeth Greenhille of Abbots Langley had 39 children – 32 daughters and seven sons, with only one set of twins. She died in 1681.

This has lots of advantages. It means we can carry our developing young around with us. We don't have to provide it with a mountain of food since the growing baby can have a proportion of the mother's intake. Because the chances of a baby protected inside its mother – and able to bounce away from predators with its running mother – are far greater than those of frogspawn abandoned in a pond, we don't have to produce as many young. We are not likely to lose so many to chance.

But it also has its downside. The baby is seen by the mother's body as an intruder, and the rejection/defence process takes a while to settle down, during which time the mother can feel pretty lousy. Nine months of growth can produce a very big passenger, and dropping them off can be a tricky and painful process. And even when the baby is born, the job is not over.

### How does it all start?

Girls and boys are much more alike than they may think! The sex organs grow from the same sort of buds – and it is more in the relative growth and size of these that we vary sexually. Equivalents of male organs can be found in the female but the way they have grown is very different. Men even have nipples, which, given another toss of the sexual dice, might have developed into breasts.

Puberty is the name given to the start of sexual development. For many girls, this is marked by the budding of their breasts and their first period. For both boys and girls, hair grows on the body, its purpose the retention of sexual scents. For boys, the hair is followed by the voice 'breaking'. Boys' vocal cords – the membranes that vibrate when we speak – grow twice as fast as girls'. Their voices become deeper. If they are lucky, the 'break' is a clean one and they quite abruptly have deeper voices. But for some boys the process is not so smooth, and they go through times when they open their mouths without knowing what will come out!

## Girls' bits

The female sex organs are mostly internal, tucked away inside the lower abdomen. The opening to the outside (the vulva) is guarded by two folds of skin called the labia. Between the labia is a sensitive organ called the clitoris. From the labia, the vagina, a muscular tube around 10cm long, points back to the bottle-shaped uterus or womb. A tiny hole connects the neck of the womb (the cervix) to the vagina. Two fallopian tubes – one each side – open into the womb. Their frilly ends are wrapped around the ovaries, where the eggs are produced.

Each month, an egg cell ripens in the ovaries. This takes two weeks, and activates a process that is called a period (menstruation). The ripe egg cell is released from the surface of the ovary and makes a journey lasting three or four days along the fallopian tube to the womb, pushed along by rippling muscles in the tube wall.

Meanwhile, the walls of the womb are getting thicker and spongier. It is preparing to receive the egg cell if it has been fertilised by a male sperm. Usually, the womb will be disappointed. The egg cell is not fertilised, and the spongy lining of the womb breaks up and is lost, together with some blood. This is the period.

Periods begin with puberty, and regular periods are experienced every 28 days or so. Periods can become irregular, and stop altogether during pregnancy or when the breasts are making milk. In later life, periods become irregular again and finally stop altogether – this is called the menopause.

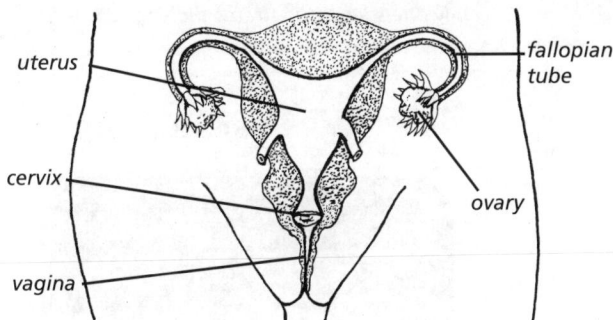

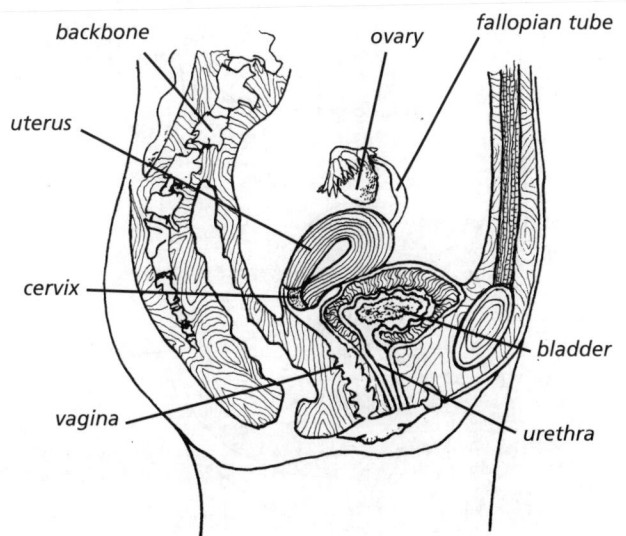

## Boys' bits

Male sex organs make special cells called sperm. Millions of them are made every day. Almost all are destined to fail, since very few will penetrate and fertilise an egg cell.

The sperm factories are called testicles. Because sperm are sensitive to temperature and cannot grow in heat, testicles usually hang outside the body. Inside these oval balls, the sperm are produced in a mass of microscopic tubes. They are pushed out of the testicles and into the prostate gland at the top of the urethra. This gland makes a white liquid that mixes with the sperm to make sticky semen. This is squirted along the penis during intercourse.

The microscopic sperm are able to swim. Their bodies are like battery packs, powering the thrashing tails. This is just as well, because each sperm faces a journey of 10cm if it is to fertilise an egg cell. But before that, the sperm have to be placed in a position where this journey is likely to be successful. They have to arrive at the cervix – the front door of the womb.

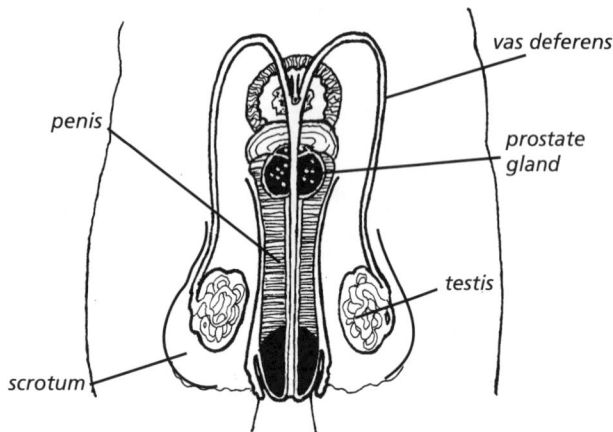

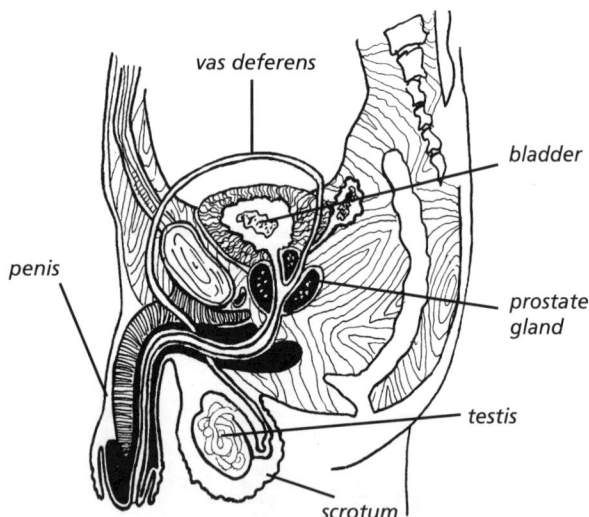

# Making a baby

First comes intercourse – the enjoyable process which includes the insertion of the man's penis into the woman's vagina. The pleasure of each other's bodies excites them both and the man's penis becomes stiff (an erection) while the woman's vagina becomes firmer. During intercourse, a few millilitres of semen are squirted into the vagina. The long swim begins.

Each sperm has to make the long journey through the tiny entrance of the womb and into one of the fallopian tubes. Then it has to find its way to the egg cell, which fortunately encourages the sperm with a homing device – a chemical so desirable that it ensures that the sperm follow it to its source. But even after the massive 10cm swim, the competition is not over. Only one sperm can combine with the egg, and there is a scrum to be that sperm. When the winning sperm breaks the egg cell membrane, this membrane changes instantly to a protective plate to keep other sperm out. The egg is fertilised, and a new human life begins.

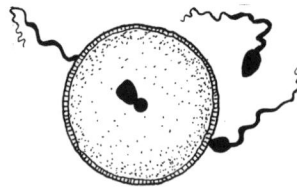

*Only one sperm penetrates the egg cell.*

Fascinating facts

- There is 1.6km of tubing in the testicles.

- Each time the penis ejects semen it produces about 4ml – containing 400 million sperm.

- Forty sperm cells could be placed head to tail across the head of a pin.

- An egg cell is smaller than a grain of salt – 0.125mm across.

- Each woman has around 400 egg cells at puberty. She will lose them, one by one, through her life.

*vas deferens*

*penis*

*prostate gland*

*testis*

*scrotum*

*vas deferens*

*bladder*

*penis*

*prostate gland*

*testis*

*scrotum*

## The growing baby

If you were to watch the whole process from now on, this is what you would see. (Opinions on exactly what happens when vary – these are guidelines to the stages of development.)

### The first stages

As the fertilised egg cell continues its journey to the womb, it splits and splits again. One cell becomes two, two become four, and four, eight. It is becoming a little growing ball of cells smaller than a pinhead.

Once in the womb, the fertilised egg cell finds a safe home in the spongy lining, and the woman is now pregnant. Some of the cells become the embryo – the future baby. It is disc-shaped – and tiny. Other cells surround the embryo and provide it with all its needs. This is the placenta – the growing baby's life support system.

### Week five

The embryo begins to lengthen. It is already possible to see a head and tail. The face and limbs develop.

### Week six

The eyes and internal organs begin to take shape. The fingers and toes are visible – but they are webbed.

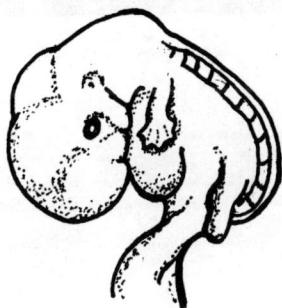

### Week twelve

The eyes now appear more to the front of the head and the hands look more like human hands. The baby is beginning to form its own male and female bits. The tail that was there at the beginning is absorbed into the body. The ears are forming.

### Weeks twelve to sixteen

During this period the baby becomes fully formed and recognisable as human. It has separate fingers and toes and the nails, eyelids, eyelashes and eyebrows have begun to form. The baby can now hear.

### Week forty

The baby is now ready for entry into the world.

## Welcome to the world

Babies are usually born about 38–40 weeks after conception. By then, the head should be resting on the cervix – the entrance to the womb. The mother's muscles begin to contract, pushing the baby out of the cervix and into the vagina. The baby is pushed head first into the world, followed by its placenta, now attached by the umbilical cord. The cord is cut – painlessly – and the end of the cord will drop off leaving the tummy button as a scar.

The baby takes a deep breath – on its own and not, usually, because it has been slapped! – and begins its independent life.

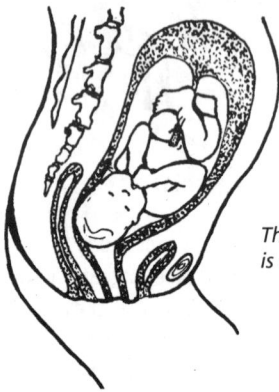

The baby's head is engaged.

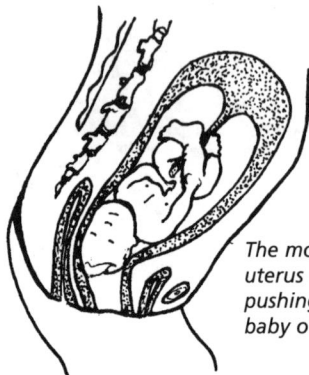

The mother's uterus contracts, pushing the baby out.

The baby is forced into the open air still attached by the umbilical cord.

## It's a long job

Mammal babies may be born out in the open, so the young of animals that live on grasslands and plains are born mature enough to fend for themselves very quickly. They have to be. There is nowhere to shelter and, while they are unable to run, they are vulnerable and at risk. So foals, for example, can get to their feet within an hour of being born. Mammals that live in nests and burrows are different. Here, the babies can be born in a less mature condition. They may be blind and hairless. They can shelter in the nest while they mature and only venture out into the world when they can run and protect themselves. Gerbils are like this and they look like pink pencil erasers for the first few days of life. Baby guinea pigs are much more appealing – furry, wide-eyed plains animals which resemble their parents.

Human babies are born totally helpless. The next few years are a process of nurture and teaching that will eventually allow them to fend for themselves. During part of that time they – like all other mammals, including whales – are fed on a nutrient called milk, that not only contains the right food balance for them but also includes antibodies from the mother to protect against disease. The whole process of growing up is slower for humans than for any other animal. There is so much to learn.

## Fascinating facts

- James Gill was the world's most premature baby, when he arrived 128 days early in Ottawa in 1987. He weighed 1lb 6oz – the same as a dozen eggs.

- 17-month-old Zack Strenkert weighed five stone at 17 months – the normal weight for a six- to 14-year-old.

# Activities

## Level One

Ask the children to order pictures of themselves and others by age or in the stages of the human life-cycle. How do the people in the pictures differ? What do the children expect to happen to them at each age? Display the pictures in order with the expectations alongside.

Relate realistic ages to the activities and expectations of the children. When will children learn to write, swim, or ride a bike?

## Level Two

You might invite a baby and toddler to school for this activity; but be sure that the toddler is happy to take part!

Compare a baby and a toddler. What can a toddler do that a baby can't? In which ways are a toddler and baby dependent upon their parents?

Ask the children to list the possibilities under the headings 'The baby can', 'The baby can't', 'The toddler can' and 'The toddler can't'. When do the children expect a baby will move to the toddler stage, and what will they do at each age and stage?

## Level Three

How do humans and other animals care for their offspring? Ask the children to compare themselves with their own pets. How are they different? How are they the same? How much care do the offspring of their pets need as they grow? How much care and attention do human babies need as they grow? Who gives this care? What do the pet and human baby expect from their parents? How do fish, hamsters, cats and dogs care for their offspring?

Ask the children to devise a handbook of care for a baby. What needs do they have? How often should those needs be met?

## Level Four

Together, consider how girls and boys are different. Discuss physical differences and changes. How will the children change as they age? Discuss the signs of puberty for boys and girls. Explain the physical changes and the importance of increased attention to hygiene.

Explore and present a resource on caring for human babies. Discuss how young people are able, physically, to produce babies, but are unprepared for parenthood. Explain why early reproduction is inappropriate (but be sensitive to family circumstances). Tell the children about the 'substitute baby' activities, where young people are asked to care for an automated baby or even a bag of sugar, for days on end. Explain that young people usually decide against early parenthood after taking part in these activities and then ask for reasons why they think this is the case.

## Level Five

Look at the structure and function of the reproductive organs in greater detail. Compare reproduction in humans with that of plants (the way that male and female cells combine to produce new life).

The children could draw and label human reproductive organs and explain the functions of each part. They could also investigate the changes brought about at puberty, for example the growth of body hair and – in boys – a breaking voice.

Look at the way that human babies vary and how this is related to inherited characteristics (being sensitive to children who may not live with their natural parents or may be unaware of their adoption).

Ask the children to explain the stages in human birth. They could produce an explanatory, illustrated brochure for a younger child entitled 'How your new brother or sister will be born'.

# How do I breathe?

There are a number of design faults in the human body but it's too late to take it back to the manufacturer, so we have to live with them. One of them is our inability to store oxygen.

## Oxygen

We need oxygen every moment of the day. Even when sitting still, doing very little or even nothing, we cannot stop the tick-over of our body systems. Our brain alone, even when we are just skimming a tabloid newspaper and it seems to be in neutral, is whirring away, demanding energy. It is a high energy user. We may notice that our heads stay hot even when the rest of us is cold. The brain is continuing to control the body processes and shuffle and back up files, and all this activity produces heat. That's why wearing a hat keeps in so much of our body heat. We are covering a major heat generator. To complete all these activities the brain needs oxygen.

We need this oxygen to break down nutrients and release energy. This is the process of respiration, and it takes place in every cell in the body. But how do the nutrients – and the oxygen – get there? And how is the waste, including carbon dioxide, taken away?

### Take a deep breath

The planet is unlikely to be invaded by giant ants. Although mammoth insects are popular with film makers, there is a limit to the size of insect bodies. That limit is how far air will travel down the tubes – called spiracles – that are their breathing organs and that open on the sides of their bodies. The air will naturally change in these tubes so long as they stay quite short. That restricts the thickness

of the fattest insect body to about that of a finger or thumb. Any fatter and the air will not reach the internal cells and the insect will die.

If you want to be bigger than an insect, you need an organ that is devoted to the exchange of gases – oxygen-rich air in, and air with more carbon dioxide in it, out. Fish have gills; other backboned animals have lungs.

Lungs are more like sponges than bags. We have two of them – one larger than the other – and they are important enough to sit inside a protective cage of bones called the ribs. They inflate and deflate and, as they do so, they pull in the air and push it out. We call this process breathing.

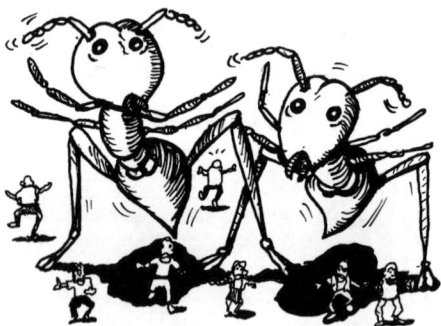

*Breathing out*

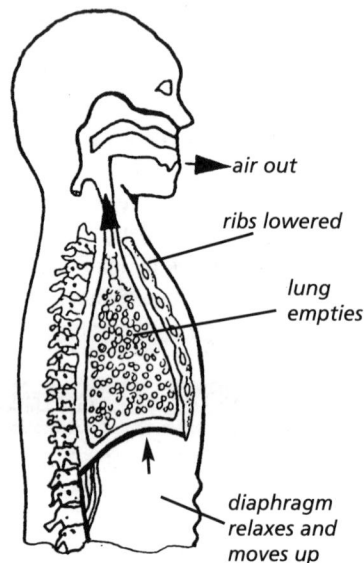

air out

ribs lowered

lung empties

diaphragm relaxes and moves up

*Breathing in*

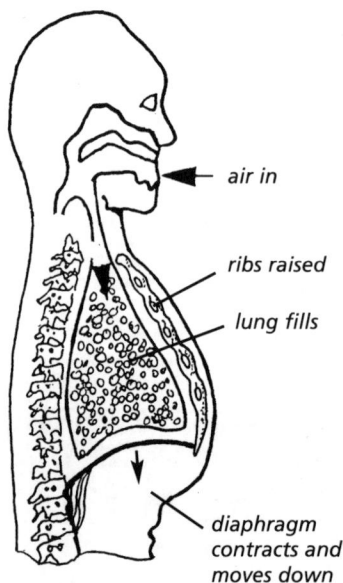

air in

ribs raised

lung fills

diaphragm contracts and moves down

We can see that our chest gets bigger and smaller when we breathe; but this is not the only way that the lungs expand and contract. A muscular drum skin called the diaphragm shuts off the bottom of the chest cavity. This drum skin can contract, becoming flat – or relax, becoming domed. This change in shape makes the lung cavity bigger and smaller. And that affects the size of the lungs.

The chest cavity – the box containing the lungs – is sealed. If it gets bigger, then there is a vacuum inside it. If it gets smaller, it puts pressure on the lungs. Because they are open to the outdoors through your nose and mouth, the lungs respond to these changes in pressure by getting bigger and smaller. Chest expands and diaphragm flattens – chest cavity bigger – lungs expand – air rushes in. Chest gets smaller – ribs press in – diaphragm becomes domed – lungs squash and air is pushed out. Breathe in; breathe out. And all without the diaphragm or the ribs touching the lungs themselves.

## The oxygen's journey

But if you are a tiny cell living contentedly in the middle of a tummy button, how is this oxygen going to get to you? The answer is that it will have to go on a bit of a journey.

The first part of the journey is in through your mouth (or your nose) and down a stiff pipe called the trachea. This branches into two bronchi – one for each lung. Now the air travels down tunnels that get narrower and narrower, branching as they go. The thinner branches – the bronchioles – go on getting thinner until each reaches a handful of small sacs – the alveoli. These look like a bunch of grapes but are in fact hollow sacs with room inside each for a spoonful of air.

In each grape – each alveolus – a little swap takes place. Oxygen-rich air goes in – carbon dioxide-rich air comes out. Not that all the oxygen is absorbed; neither is all the gas breathed out carbon dioxide. The air you breathe out is a tiny bit different from the air you breathed in. Less oxygen; more carbon dioxide.

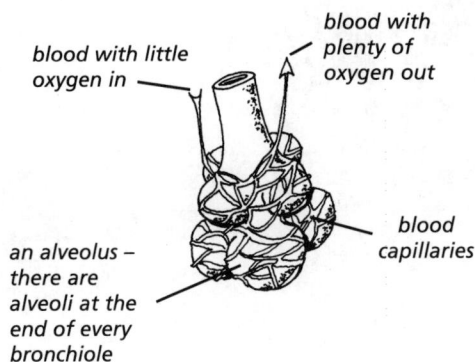

## Fascinating facts

- You take around 600 million breaths in your life, taking in about six litres of air every minute.

- Average resting breathing is 13–17 breaths a minute. You may take 80 breaths a minute during vigorous exercise. New-born babies breathe 40 times a minute.

- There are 300 million alveoli in your lungs.

- You breathe about 15 cubic metres of air a day – enough to fill a small room or six phone boxes.

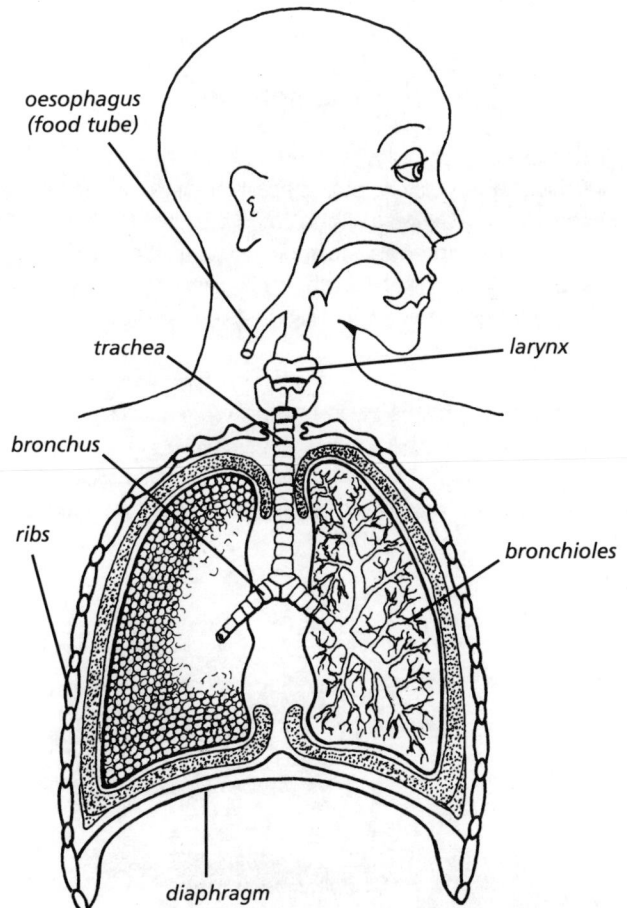

oesophagus
(food tube)

trachea

larynx

bronchus

ribs

bronchioles

diaphragm

blood with little oxygen in

blood with plenty of oxygen out

blood capillaries

an alveolus – there are alveoli at the end of every bronchiole

One grapeful may not seem like much oxygen but there are millions of alveoli – so many that someone has calculated that, spread out, they would cover a complete tennis court.

And the oxygen you've taken in? Well, that gets whipped away by the circulatory system (see Chapter 6) and eventually arrives at that lonely cell in the tummy button, where it is welcomed to enable that cell to respire.

## Hold it!

Most of us only use a small proportion of our lungs in our everyday breathing. We rarely breathe deeply, except after exercise, when the build-up of waste products in our bodies demands a few deep breaths to get rid of the carbon dioxide and recharge us with oxygen. The lower parts of our lungs may not get ventilated very often, which is one reason why a bit of exercise and some occasional 'getting out of breath' can be good for us. Of course, some of us abuse these wonderful organs by filling the tunnels and sacs with smoke. A sure way to do them harm! (See Chapter 7.)

## Breathing under water

There was once a goldfish who was determined to breathe air. Every day he put his head out of the water for a moment or two. Eventually he could breathe air for so long that he could climb a rung or two up a little ladder that rose out of the water. Each day he climbed higher. At last he reached the very top rung. Disaster! He slipped, fell and was drowned.

Most fish can't breathe air, and mammals like us can't breathe under water. A whale is a mammal, and it can't breathe under water. It will dive to a considerable depth, taking with it the oxygen it needs for around half an hour

### Fascinating facts

- You can hold your breath for about a minute. A bottle-nosed whale can hold its breath for two hours.

- You have a flap in your throat that ensures that food doesn't go down your windpipe.

- You cough to get rid of something irritating in your air tubes and lungs. A cough can let the air out at 100kph.

- The air you breathe in contains about 0.04 per cent carbon dioxide. The air you breathe out contains about 4 per cent.

of activity before coming to the surface again, blowing off the carbon dioxide it has accumulated, taking in great draughts of oxygen and diving again.

We can only do this to a limited extent. We can take a deep breath and go under water. With training, we can hold our breath for some minutes and make use of the oxygen in our blood and tissues. But pretty soon, we are going to run out and the carbon dioxide is going to build up and send messages to the brain saying 'Take a breath!' and then we need to get to the air – quick!

GET OUT QUICK!

# Activities

## Level One

Ask the children to talk about their breathing and how it varies in different circumstances. We breathe deeply when exercising. We take deep breaths when swimming (but not under water). We take a deep breath before diving or jumping in.

Establish that we need air to live, and that we cannot breathe under water. This is an opportunity to discuss the dangers of plastic bags, deep water and play that includes 'choking'. All could be lethal.

## Level Two

Discuss why we need air to live. Establish that we need air for activity; that we take in air and change it and then breathe out the changed air.

Ask the children to do different activities and record the changes in their breathing; but note that breathing is directly under our control and that they can voluntarily take more – or fewer – breaths than they need. Discuss their discoveries. When do we breathe faster and slower? What do we mean when we say 'out of breath'? Why do we take deep breaths when we are frightened? Is it to prepare us for fight or flight? Why does excitement leave us 'breathless'?

## Level Three

Ask the children to research the function of their lungs. What do the ribs and diaphragm do? They can model the function of the lungs by modelling the chest cavity.

Cut the base off a small plastic bottle (the chest). Plug the neck with Plasticine and push a small tube through it (the trachea) that has a balloon (the lungs) tightly fixed to the end. Close the base of the bottle tightly with a sheet of burst balloon (the diaphragm). Pull the centre of the diaphragm. This reduces the pressure in the chest and the lungs should expand. Release the diaphragm and the lungs will return to normal. Discuss why a puncture of the chest can lead to a lung collapsing. Point out that this is why the chest is so well protected with a cage of ribs.

## Level Four

Investigate the connection between exercise and breathing rate. As before, note that breathing is directly under our control and that children can voluntarily take more – or fewer – breaths than they need.

Record baseline breathing rate, the rate immediately after exercise, and how quickly breathing returns to normal. Note that the speed of return to base breathing rate is one measure of fitness. Ask children to be as honest as possible about their need for breaths. It is easy to take far too many (to gasp and wheeze). This affects the readings.

## Level Five

Look at the structure and function of the lungs in greater detail. Look at the microscopic structure. With proper safety precautions, you might show the children the lungs or lights from a butcher's; or you could demonstrate the lungs' spongy structure with a model.

The children can draw and label the lungs and explain the functions of each part of the respiratory system.

With their permission, you could involve affected children in the class in a discussion about asthma and how they overcome it. In asthma, the bronchi, usually as wide as hosepipes, can close down to the thickness of drinking straws. This makes breathing extremely difficult. The children could explain how they use inhalers to prevent or treat this condition. Many of them have learnt to overcome panic and to control the symptoms without drugs. Point out that these children are able to compete successfully in sports, and live a normal life.

# How do I see, hear, smell, taste and touch?

**By 'senses' we mean the five ways in which we experience things around us. These senses are all receivers. We do not see or hear actively. We collect the light in our eyes and the sound in our ears.**

This is a very mature concept and goes against everything we commonly say, for example 'He gave it a piercing look,' 'She peered through the fog,' and 'I can see through this window.' You might not expect children to accept it all at once, but with experience it can be understood.

We can, however, focus on a particular sense or sensation. You can listen intently, or look closely at something; you can focus on a particular sensation – sniffing a particular scent, experiencing a pleasant taste, enjoying being patted or cuddled.

## A sixth sense?

We usually reckon to have five senses. They are seeing, hearing, smelling, tasting and touching. You can argue that we have one more – a 'sixth sense' that tells us about things we don't immediately experience, perhaps. There is also a sense – or combination of senses – that tells us whether we are the right way up. This can be confused, if we are buried in snow, for example, or floating in water with no light to help us recognise up.

Children should recognise the five senses with help. Some of them commonly work together – taste and smell, for example – and this can complicate understanding.

## Superman sees with magic beams

If children look at a bright light bulb (not for long!) they can recognise that light from the bulb is coming to their eyes. But if they look at something that is not a light source, they don't understand that the light has to be reflected from it for them to see it. It isn't a bright light, so how do you see it? Many children will answer that they see with a beam of light from their own eyes, like Superman!

These ideas are very firmly held and, while the facts may challenge them, you cannot expect to 'convert' children to the accepted science in every case.

Young children may not connect the ear with hearing at all. They may believe that they hear a sound 'Because I was listening,' and they can believe in an active ear rather than a passive receiver.

Less research has been done into what children think about the other senses – although most of them recognise that they have a brain while a doll does not. Only older children associate the brain with the senses.

So how do these senses actually work?

# How do we see?

Well, we don't send out rays from our eyes like Superman. Our eyes are receptors of light – they passively take in the light that falls on them.

We see when light enters our eyes. Our eyes are organs that are sensitive to the visible range of the electromagnetic spectrum, and they are adapted to allow a reasonable amount of light to enter – the iris closing the pupil in bright light, or opening it in low light. We cannot see without a light source. Even in the low light level of a darkened room we may still be able to see a little; in total darkness we can see nothing.

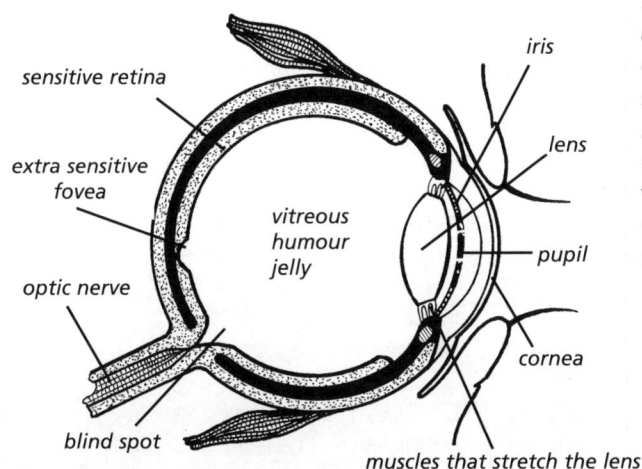

*sensitive retina*
*extra sensitive fovea*
*optic nerve*
*blind spot*
*iris*
*lens*
*vitreous humour jelly*
*pupil*
*cornea*
*muscles that stretch the lens*

We see light sources – like candles and torches. We see objects because light from a light source is reflected into our eyes. We see because light passes through transparent materials and (with difficulty) through translucent ones. We can also see images reflected in mirrors. Because light is reflected directly back at us by a mirror, we see the world reversed. Our left pocket is reflected back to our left, and so appears to be on the right when we look at the image.

## It's all upside-down

The picture that forms on the back of your eye is actually upside-down. Your brain quickly learns to turn the picture the right way up when you are a baby – though until you've picked up this trick, you may be grabbing for things hanging above your cot and missing.

A scientist tried wearing glasses that inverted his view, and eventually his brain got used to the idea of everything being the wrong way up. His brain made the necessary adaptation, and he was able to see things correctly again. Then he took the glasses off …

Amazingly, eyes have evolved more than once to the same design in the animal kingdom. The big molluscs – octopuses and squid – have eyes very like our own, with a lens.

## Seeing in colour

There are five to seven million cones in each eye. These are special receptors that respond to blue, green and red light and they enable us to see in colour. They work best in bright light. When the light levels dip too low, the rods take over. They can work in dim light, detecting movement and shape. The 120 million or more rods allow us to see in half-darkness.

Some people – often men – are born 'colour-blind'. They are actually deficient in distinguishing some colours, especially red and green. This has made them much more sensitive to subtle colour differences and to movement. Men with this characteristic made better hunters when seeking out deer and other camouflaged animals in woodland. Colour vision deficient men were especially chosen as snipers in World War I. But colour vision deficiency is a nuisance when matching a shirt and tie!

## Fascinating facts

- Many insects can see ultraviolet light; some snakes can see heat. Snakes also use their tongues to flick smells back into their mouths.

- Some animals can sense light with a third eye – the pineal – on the top of their heads. They use it to track day length and the changing seasons.

- 20/20 vision is the ability to see at 20 feet what a normal eye can see at that distance. Some people see even better. 20/15 means that you can see at 20 feet what most people see at 15.

- Many newborn babies have blue eyes. The amount of melanin pigment in the iris determines our eye colour. Over several months, melanin moves to the surface of some babies' eyes, changing their colour.

# How do we hear?

Children have wide experience of making and hearing sound. They seldom have any great idea of how sound is made, or why they can hear it and there is no reason why they should. Look at this diagram showing the inside of the ear.

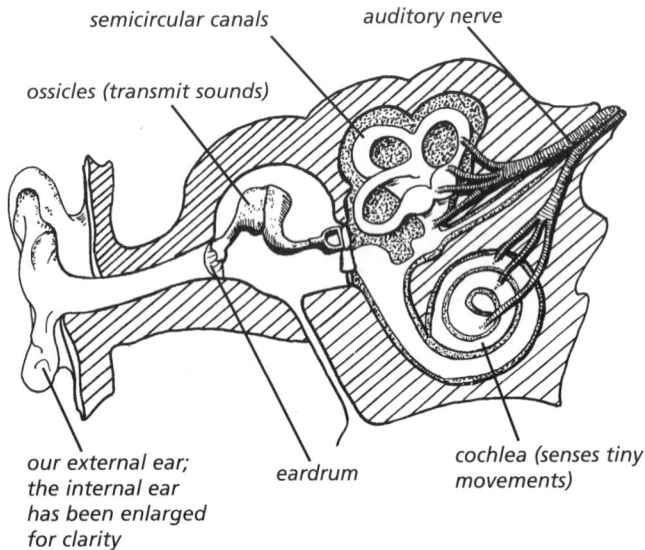

semicircular canals  auditory nerve

ossicles (transmit sounds)

our external ear; the internal ear has been enlarged for clarity

eardrum

cochlea (senses tiny movements)

Sound is produced when something vibrates. The vibrations may be tiny – or large enough to see. The vibrations are transmitted through the air and also through water and through solid objects too. It is soft, absorbent materials that insulate against sound.

We hear sounds when vibrations in the air reach our ear. Sound waves are vibrations of the air. They make the eardrum vibrate and these vibrations are amplified and transmitted through the three earbones (ossicles) to the cochlea. The stirrup works like a piston, vibrating the fluid in the cochlea. Sense cells in the cochlea feel this movement and transmit nerve messages to the brain. We interpret these as sounds.

Our brains are programmed to receive sounds. We recognise familiar voices and can pick them out from a noisy room. We can even recognise familiar sounds from the smallest amount of evidence – a piece of music from the first notes. We enjoy hearing music played in tune while a slightly out-of-tune piece makes us laugh or groan. A badly-played piece may be almost painful. There is something about the pattern and predictability of music that makes it enjoyable.

Because of our programming, we may find it difficult to appreciate music from cultures other than our own. Balinese temple music, with its bell sounds, may be a cacophony to us. We have to learn to appreciate other forms of music and, in particular, to pick out the 'voices' of different instruments. You can pick out a single instrument easily in an orchestra but you would have trouble with a piece of electronic music. That is why electronic musicians tend to add the 'voices' one by one. The classic example is the record 'Tubular Bells'.

Our ear is also sensitive to gravity, giving us information that helps us to orientate ourselves. The semicircular canals, at right angles to each other, monitor our movements and help us to keep our balance.

### I don't shout so loud when my hands are over my ears

Children have difficulties with the nature and language of sound. It's a common misconception that covering your ears actually makes your voice quieter – that's the effect on you, after all.

They also confuse volume and pitch. Ask a young child to sing higher, and they may sing louder.

There are sounds beyond our range of hearing – both high and low. Children will have the ability to hear very high sounds. With age, tissues become less flexible and the transmission of sound through our ears declines. The tiny, rapid vibrations of high sounds are the first to be lost. Interestingly, hearing impaired musicians, like Evelyn Glennie, the percussionist, may be able to relate to vibrations of which normally-hearing people are unaware.

You can learn a great deal from percussion instruments – tuned (xylophones and chime bars) and untuned (cymbals and drums). A tuning fork will produce a clearly discernible vibration. A 'slinky' or wire helix will show one idea of how sound waves travel – but it's a very imperfect picture.

## Fascinating facts

- Two synthetic chemicals – ethyl mercaptan and butyl seleno-mercaptan – are among the most disgusting to be created. They combine rotting cabbage, garlic and sewer gas.

- A West African plant produces a material that is a thousand times sweeter than sugar.

- Research suggests that our noses may be sensitive to magnetism, giving us a sense of direction.

- The female atlas moth uses a chemical to advertise when she is ready to mate. The male can sense it with his huge antennae as far as 8km away.

# What's that smell?

Our sense of smell is very sensitive, though not a patch on the senses of animals like dogs or some butterflies that can trace a mate by smell from miles away. People whose work depends on smell – perfume makers, coffee and tea importers – can sense many thousands of different odours. A dog is a million times more sensitive than a human to smells. But all these smells are built from seven basic smells in different combinations of intensity.

The seven recognised smells are:

- ethereal
- floral
- mothball
- musk
- peppermint
- pungent
- putrid

We recognise these because we have seven different types of sensor cells. The 'organ' of smell is the lining of your nose – mostly a patch of hairy sensor cells on the roof of your nose. The sensor cells are covered with tiny hairs and a sticky jelly that captures the smell molecules from the air. Each of the sensor cells responds to one of these kinds of smells. The smell fits the sensor cell like a key fits a lock. The combination of smells reported by the smell cells is sent to the brain. The brain interprets the messages and recognises the food, flowers or other source.

The sense of smell is very evocative. It seems to have a hot line to stored memories. So a smell – more than any other sense – will trigger memories and remind us of somewhere distant in time or place.

# What's that taste?

Your sense of smell makes your sense of taste a great deal more accurate. Smells from your food reach your nose while you are eating. When you have a cold, your nose is blocked and your food tastes dull. That's because the sticky mucus we all produce when we have a cold masks the smell cells.

Your tongue is covered with taste cells or 'buds'. These are cells with small hairs. Different tastes fit these chemically. A 'sour' cell and lemon juice fit together like a lock and a key. The taste bud signals the brain – 'That's a lemon,' and the brain takes that information and mixes it with information from the nose which has smelled oils from the lemon peel and flesh. 'Yup,' says the brain, 'that's a lemon all right!'

This is why we are surprised when information from different senses contradicts our experience. We associate blue-black food with blackcurrant and get a shock when a blue-black drink in the USA tastes of grapes.

The number of taste buds varies widely from individual to individual, with some – especially women – having many times more than others. There are four basic types of taste buds. Different areas of your tongue have more of each kind – the tip of your tongue is more sensitive to sweet and salty tastes, the sides to sour tastes and the base or back to bitter tastes. The bitter buds work for longer than the others, which is why you may have a bitter taste in your mouth for a long time after eating. The smell and taste centres in your brain are very close together, which is another reason why we enjoy our food better if we can smell it.

# A sense of touch

Your body is covered in millions of nerve endings that are sensitive to different forms of stimuli – touch, heat, cold, pressure and pain. Depending on which part of the body these nerve endings are on, there are greater or lesser numbers. Our lips and fingertips, for example, have far more detectors than the small of our back. Consequently, our fingers can do more sensitive things – like picking things up.

**The least sensitive part of our body is our bottom – just as well, or we would find sitting down very uncomfortable!**

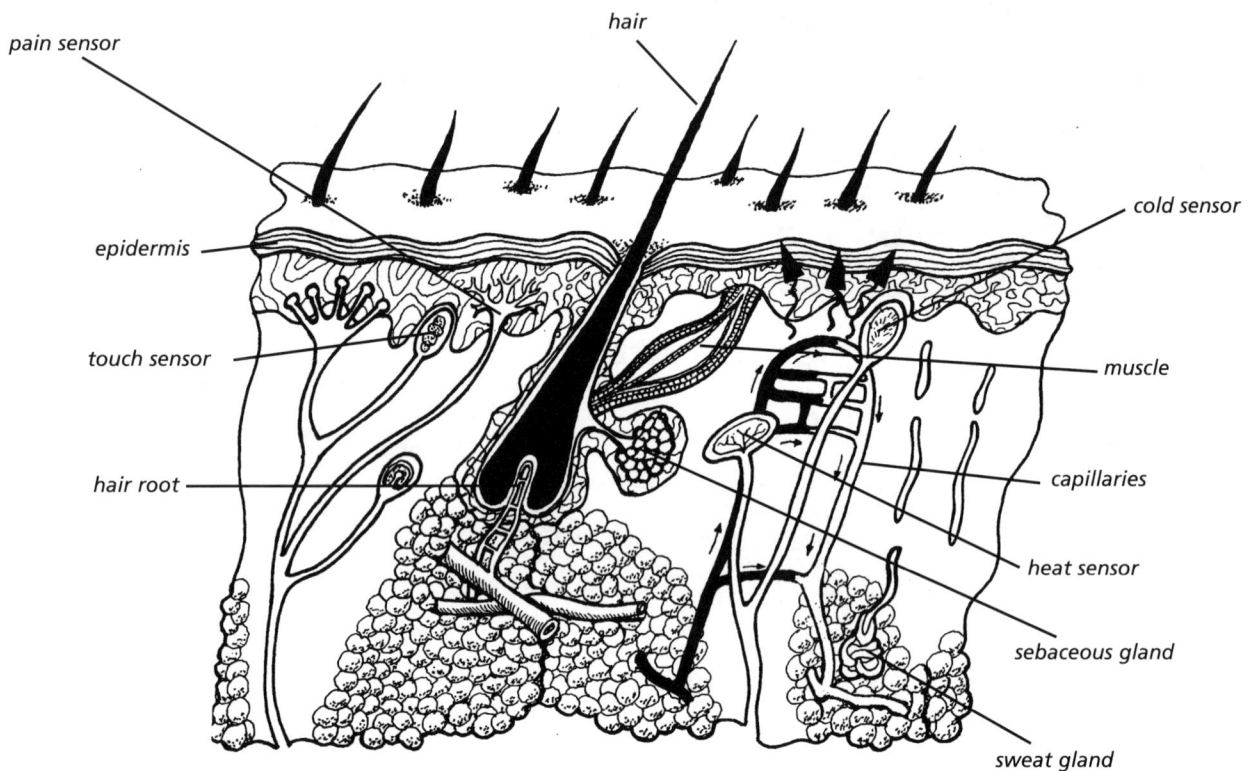

pain sensor

hair

cold sensor

epidermis

touch sensor

muscle

hair root

capillaries

heat sensor

sebaceous gland

sweat gland

## Fascinating facts

- Chocolate contains 300 chemicals, some of which act like drugs. Its melting point is close to human body temperature, so that it softens on your tongue.

- Some animals are sensitive to electricity, underwater vibration and the tiny ground vibrations before earthquakes.

- The giant squid has an eye over a foot in diameter – 120 times bigger than ours.

- Chameleons can look in two directions at once.

- Dogs and squirrels cannot distinguish red and green, and see in blues and yellows.

# Activities

## Level One

Ask children to identify and explain the function of each of the five senses. Make posters to show these. Discuss the ways that people live with deficiencies or loss of some of these senses. Children may have personal experience, or know of people who have overcome sensory difficulties.

## Level Two

Investigate the senses of taste and smell and how they are related. The children could try identifying foods hidden in smell pots, or taste foods while blindfolded. Who can identify the food they are eating while holding their nose? Children will commonly identify smells by the foods they know – so onion might be called 'burger' and herbs may be called 'pizza'. Show them the correct answers and discuss how they decided on their answers.

Discuss the safety advantages of a good sense of smell and taste.

## Level Three

Investigate touch. Can two blunt pin-pricks a short distance apart be distinguished from a single pin-prick on the fingertip, back or leg? Which parts of the body are more sensitive? Why might some parts of the body be more sensitive than others?

Ask the children to find out why some parts of the body are more sensitive than others. Why are the fingertips and lips so sensitive? Discuss the need to handle things with care, and the need to sense food going into the mouth.

Point out that babies put things in their mouths simply because this is a very sensitive part of the body. Other parts of the body are (fortunately) less sensitive. Walking and sitting would both be very uncomfortable if our feet and bottoms were more pressure sensitive.

## Level Four

Explore hearing. Can sounds be identified? Can their direction be determined when we are blindfolded? Are both ears needed for this? Can direction be determined with one ear? How sensitive is hearing to small sounds?

The children should find that sounds are easily identified, and so is the direction they are coming from. We are not as dependent upon both ears as we might think. We can usually identify the direction of a sound with one ear only.

Explore children's understanding of hearing (we hear because our ears are receivers). Remind them of the importance of hearing linked to safety. For example, walking along or cycling with a hood up, earflaps down, wearing Walkman headphones, or a phone held to one ear. All reduce the signals we get from the world around us and this puts us at risk.

## Level Five

Investigate sight. How well can signs be read with increasing distance? Do the colours make a difference? Explain that contrasts are best seen at a distance, for example black on yellow. Ask the children to explain how they think their eyes work. Look for the accepted model (that our eyes are receivers of reflected light).

Point out that our eyes receive light, but our brains make sense of it, even filling in the 'blind spot' in our picture where the optic nerve enters the retina. This is why our eyes are constantly moving, scanning and constructing a picture of our surroundings.

Investigate the area that each eye can see. One child rests their chin on a sheet of paper on the table and looks at a distant object. If they close one eye and a pencil is swept in an arc around their head, then the furthest they can see to left and right can be marked on the paper for each eye. The result is two big, overlapping areas. The central zone – seen by both eyes – is the area of 3-D vision.

Introduce the structure of the eye and ear. Challenge the children to name the parts and their functions. Define the differences between the colour-sensitive cone cells and the shade-sensitive rods in the eye.

Investigate optical illusions and the way in which the eyes and brain are connected. Explain that the brain is the interpreter of what we see. It is the brain's interpretation of the eye's messages that is confused by optical illusions. The brain is looking for patterns that may not be there.

# Why do I need blood?

## Why do we have blood?

**What is this mysterious stuff that drips out when we cut ourselves? Many young children suspect that we are large bags of this red liquid, and we leak like a punctured carrier bag. The truth is a little different.**

### Room service! The functions of blood

The blood system is the body's main means of transport. Blood carries nutrients and oxygen to each and every cell, and takes away the waste products. Like room service in a hotel with a billion rooms, the blood system sees that each cell gets the attention it needs. All backboned animals – fish, reptiles, amphibians, birds and mammals – have blood. Some invertebrates or minibeasts have blood systems too.

Like good room service, blood also has a security function, carrying the body's police to any scenes of disruption.

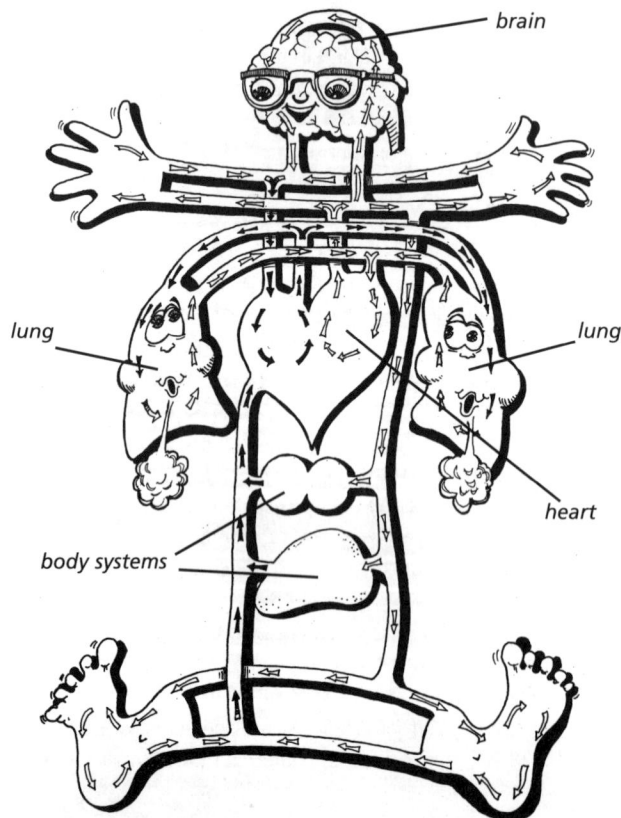

### Fascinating facts

- There are around six million red blood cells in a single drop of your blood. You are constantly making more in your bone marrow – another ten million new ones every second. They have a tough life of about four months, being hammered round your blood vessels before the liver and spleen remove the worn and weary ones. You lose them in your body waste, which gives it a brown colour.

- During those four months, each red blood cell will make around 172,000 journeys round your body.

brain

lung

lung

heart

body systems

Your blood system carries oxygen to your tissues which is needed for the breakdown of food to release energy – a process we call respiration. You need energy all the time, just to tick over – a surprising amount of it is used by our brains, which is why your head gets hot and you can lose a lot of heat from it.

But it is when we exercise that we really make demands on our food reserves and, since we can't store it in our bodies, we need to obtain a lot more oxygen. So,
- we breathe more deeply and our heart pumps faster, sending the dissolved oxygen round our bodies;
- we produce more waste;
- the amount of carbon dioxide in our exhaled breath rises.

We are aware of these changes because of our gasping and our increased pulse rate.

### How much blood?

A small woman has about three litres of blood and a large man around five litres of blood in their body. Blood makes up one-twentieth of your body weight. The clear, watery plasma of your blood carries three sorts of passengers.

## The blood cells

First are the red cells – five billion (5 000 000 000 000) of them in every litre of blood! They are shaped like sugar-free Polos – round like a doughnut, but with a membrane across the hole. These carry the oxygen around the body.

Next are the white cells. These are different shapes, but many look like an amoeba. They are the body's security system and they act either by overcoming – even swallowing – intruders, or by making chemicals that destroy invading germs.

Finally there are tiny blood platelets. These come into their own when you cut yourself. Then they rush to hold hands across the wound, slowing the flow by forming a blood clot.

### Why aren't you cold-blooded?

Animals – including ourselves – aren't simply 'warm-blooded' or 'cold-blooded'. The so-called warm-blooded animals keep a constant body temperature. If your body temperature falls, you have to burn food to get warm again. This generates heat, and you warm up your blood and body.

Cold-blooded animals are as warm or cold as their surroundings. If you are cold-blooded, like many simpler animals, then you depend on the heat of the Sun to make you active.

## Fascinating facts

- Your red blood cells contain a chemical called haemoglobin. This can form a casual attachment to oxygen, picking it up in the lungs and dropping it off in all the cells of your body.

- This chemical – haemoglobin – makes your blood red because it is made with iron. The same chemical is found in the blood of all other backboned animals and some invertebrates too. But worms may have green blood; and lobsters and crabs, blue.

- The commonest human blood groups are O+ and A+. The rarest is called Bombay Blood and has been found in only three people – two of them a brother and sister.

- All your blood vessels, put end to end, would stretch for nearly a hundred thousand kilometres.

- Pictures suggest that blood with oxygen in it is red, and blood without oxygen is blue. That's not quite true. Oxygenated blood is bright red; blood without oxygen is dark red, but it looks blue seen through your skin in places like your wrists. You never see that purplish blood of course because the moment you cut yourself, the blood picks up oxygen from the air and looks bright red.

If a cold-blooded animal finds itself in a chilly environment, like this spider in the fridge, its body processes slow down.

In the same situation, a warm-blooded animal like you makes every effort to keep warm – energetically jumping up and down, flailing your arms and shivering. Shivering gets all the tiny muscles in your skin active, releasing energy as heat. It helps keep your body temperature steady.

Human blood is normally at a temperature of 37° Celsius. Keeping your blood – and your body – warm is a way of keeping the chemical reactions of the body working quickly, so that you can be active.

## What happens when you cut yourself?

It's never straightforward when a pipe springs a leak. And it's the same with your body. The emergency plumbers are the platelets. They become sticky, sticking to each other and the burst pipe to make a plug. They can't hold the leak for long, and they call for a mesh of fine threads from the blood which cover the wound, forming a jelly. The jelly hardens in the air to become a scab. Under the scab your body goes about repairing itself.

It is possible to bleed to death in less than a minute if a large blood vessel is broken. Losing more than two litres of blood is usually fatal.

## Fascinating facts

- William Harvey, who first discovered the way the heart works and published a book on it in 1628, calculated that your heart pumps 259 litres of blood every hour. It will beat more than two million times in your lifetime, pumping 500 million gallons of blood.

- Your heart beat at 120 beats a minute when you were a baby; it beats at 70–80 beats a minute for an adult – the lower end of the range for a resting woman and the upper end for a resting man. Athletes have really slow heart rates because their hearts are so strong that they pump in one beat what most hearts pump in two. Some cycling champs have a heart rate as low as 30 beats a minute – one every two seconds – 'lub-dup, lub-dup'.

- Earthworms have ten hearts. Animal hearts beat at different rates from yours: a horse at 48 beats a minute, a dog between 90 and 100, and a mouse at 500 beats a minute – at rest.

## So what does your heart actually do?

The engine room of your body's supply system is your heart. It is a ball of muscle about the size of your fist.

Your heart is a pump that pushes the blood round your body. Around 70 grams of blood from your lungs and from your body enters separate waiting rooms in the top of your heart. From there it passes through one-way valves into the main pump room, which forces it out at high pressure into the lungs and into every part of your body.

Your blood travels through a figure of eight. Your heart has two waiting rooms – called auricles – and these feed into the two muscular chambers called ventricles through non-return valves. The squeeze of these powerful ventricles pumps the blood around your body. Out from the right side of your heart to the lungs to pick up oxygen, and then back to the left side of your heart for a huge push to all the rest of your body.

The left ventricle has a bigger, tougher job to do than the right, and so it is much bigger, giving your heart an unbalanced look.

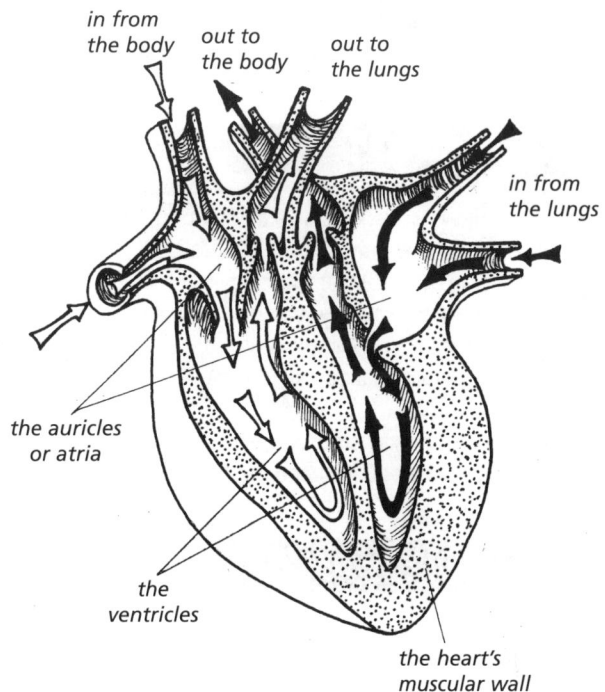

*in from the body*

*out to the body*

*out to the lungs*

*in from the lungs*

*the auricles or atria*

*the ventricles*

*the heart's muscular wall*

The arteries (thick-walled pipes) that carry your blood branch into smaller arteries and then into tiny capillaries. The blood from those fine capillaries returns to the heart through thin-walled veins.

In your lungs, the blood loses waste carbon dioxide and picks up more oxygen for respiration. (How it does this is explained in Chapter 4.)

## Fascinating facts

- Your heart is not on the left of your body. It is in the centre, quite high up; but the left side is much bigger than the right and so your heart appears to lean to your left.

- Your heart is made from muscle that will go on beating without instructions from your brain.

- The valves in your heart pop open and then slam shut with a sound that the doctor hears as a 'lub-dup, lub-dup' noise. Your pulse is a pressure wave that you can feel in your wrist and other parts of your body, like a ripple when you throw a stone in a pond.

- If you could sit on your heart and let its pumping lift you into the air, it would lift you 300 metres into the sky in a day.

# Activities

## Level One

Investigate the children's basic understanding of their circulatory system. Where is their heart? Where does their blood go? Question the idea that the body is a 'bag of blood'. You might ask the children to draw their idea of the circulatory system, and compare it with the correct picture (there are tubes and a central pump).

Ask the children how they should deal with small cuts and scrapes. Why? Talk about hygiene and health.

## Level Two

Explain that the blood is the body's transport system. Look at the different things carried in the blood and why they are important to the body.

Explore, without measuring, changes in the circulation with exercise, for example a faster heart rate, skin flushing and a thumping pulse. Ask the children to record the changes in themselves with exercise. They could draw themselves twice – once before and once after exercise – recording differences in how they look and feel.

## Level Three

Explore, count and record changes to the body with exercise. Measure the change in heart rate and the pulse. Compare this before and after exercise. Offer some explanations as to why this should be, such as a greater need for energy and greater amounts of waste products.

The body needs energy that must be delivered quickly. It produces waste that must be removed quickly. Relate this to an increased heart rate.

Children have difficulty finding their pulse. They can use their fingertips (not their thumb because this has a pulse of its own) in the small valley at the base of their hand. They can also feel a pulse on their temples close to the hairline, or, without pressing, in their necks.

## Level Four

Identify the heart, arteries and veins and explain the purpose of each. Ask the children to draw simplified pictures of the blood and the circulatory system. Investigate the effects of (safe) exercise on the pulse rate; does the rate increase with the degree of exercise? How quickly do we recover from the effects of exercise? How is this related to 'fitness'?

Children may find that some of them recover from exercise very quickly. If they graph their heart and breathing rates before and immediately after exercise, they will find that both have increased; but fitness is demonstrated by a rapid recovery to normal levels.

## Level Five

The children can explore and illustrate the structure of the heart and explain the purpose of the chambers and how the heart functions. They could present their findings as annotated pictures, or use ICT to show the stages in the beating of the heart and the flow of blood. There are models available which show the flow of blood through the heart. You can draw a heart on the playground and play hopscotch through it, for example the children hop in from the body, out to the lungs, back to the heart again and finally off to the body once more. Are they hopping into the correct side of the heart? Are they carrying lots of oxygen or lots of carbon dioxide?

Ask them to devise some basic health rules for a healthy heart.

Ask the children to research blood cells (their types and functions). Relate the respiration of cells to the need for increased blood flow and the raised pulse rate to exercise. They should relate flushing to the loss of heat during exercise.

# How do we damage our bodies?

**Our children are growing up in a world that surrounds them with body images and physical extremes. From super-waif models to muscle-bound sportsmen, children are exposed to apparent ideals that few of them are likely to achieve. Society is obsessed with healthy living to the point that immortality seems attainable. And 'diet' is an issue, not a word for balanced and sensible eating, but for constant weight regulation or loss.**

It is not surprising if some people feel that unless they achieve unattainable standards of physical health and fitness, implausible levels of happiness and perfect partners, they have somehow missed out on all that life has to offer. It is not surprising that anorexia, bulimia and other eating disorders are experienced by children as young as primary age.

Diet is an issue addressed in Chapter 1, but the effects of chemicals on the body need attention. It is not an easy area to tackle. Many of us use everyday drugs – chocolate, caffeine and alcohol are addictive.

There is money to be made from addiction. Drug misuse can lead young people from alcohol to other drugs. Some children may use solvents – glues, butane, petrol, aerosols, dry cleaner or typewriter correction fluids or nail varnish remover. 150 young people die every year from using these. Solvent abuse is a sad activity – it is both addictive and harmful.

What is addiction? Can anyone afford to lose their self control? If you tackle drug education you may find yourself addressing the whole issue of self-awareness and self-image, and asking the children 'Is this how you want others to see you?' Take smoking, for example.

## Smoking and health

Successive governments have always had very clear targets to reduce ill health and death caused by cancer and other conditions associated with the use of tobacco, by reducing the prevalence of smoking and the use of tobacco throughout the population.

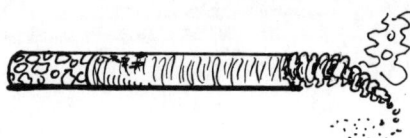

A recent government paper once aimed to:
- reduce the death rate for lung cancer by at least 30 per cent in men under 75 and 15 per cent in women under 75 by 2001
- reduce the prevalence of smoking in men and women aged 16 and over so that it is no more than 20 per cent by the year 2000
- stop at least a third of women from smoking during pregnancy
- reduce consumption of cigarettes by at least 40 per cent by the year 2000
- reduce the prevalence of smoking among 11- to 15-year-olds by at least 33 per cent.

(Figures taken from 'Fit for the Future' a Second Progress Report on the Health of the Nation, published in July, 1995.)

How many of these aims have been met? We have seen (in particular) an increase in young women smoking and many of them continue to smoke during pregnancy. There is evidence that many smokers start young – in primary school.

Unfortunately, children see smoking in films, on stage and television. Smoking in advertisements is banned, but subtle, iconic tobacco advertisements that mean little to non-smokers continue to fill the hoardings. Smoking can be seen as a sign of maturity and sophistication.

Around 10 per cent of boys and 12 per cent of girls between 11 and 15 smoke regularly, and the figures remain steady. Why are they attracted to smoking? What can be done to reduce the levels in the way that adult levels are falling? There are high levels of smoking among young women, and reasons given include looking good, feeling confident and keeping weight down. These levels have been high since the Second World War. Women risk cancer of the cervix from smoking as well as lung cancer.

Smoking also causes a fivefold increase in the risk of dying from chronic bronchitis and emphysema, and a twofold increase in deaths from diseases of the heart and coronary arteries. It increases the risk of stroke by 50 per cent – 40 per cent among men and 60 per cent among women. There is clear evidence that smoking during pregnancy can reduce birth weight and can damage babies. There have been suggestions of links between homes with smokers and cot deaths.

# How to attack smoking

Discuss tobacco dependency – tell the children about the likelihood of disease and premature death. Unfortunately, giving them this information is unlikely to have any immediate effect since young people have a sense of immortality.

Look at the statistics. Consider a thousand young people in the age range you teach. As many as six may die in road accidents, but if all smoked, 250 would die of smoking-related diseases!

How good are your children at recognising wordless icons and graphics from tobacco adverts? Deconstruct the adverts. Try using the advertising weapon against tobacco.

Consider cost. Smoking is not cheap. What else could you do with the money? Smoking for life costs the same as a Ferrari or ten trips to Florida.

Discuss why tobacco isn't banned. It would be, were it newly developed today.

Look at image, especially the link between girls and smoking and the cigarette as a fashion accessory. Ask why girls don't give up with the same success as boys. This may relate to changes in body chemistry. Remind the children of tobacco's effects on teeth, skin and hair.

**Note**
Remember that when talking about smoking, teachers need to be aware that parents and other relatives and friends may smoke. It is important not to raise children's anxiety about premature death unnecessarily.

## Just another drink – alcohol dependency

Alcohol is an acceptable, social drug. Because it is so everyday, we may overlook the downside. Alcoholism usually develops over a period of years. Early symptoms include placing excessive importance on having alcohol to hand. Ensuring this availability influences the person's choice of associates or activities. Alcohol comes to be used more as a mood-changing drug than as a foodstuff or beverage served as a part of social custom or religious ritual.

## A few facts

- **Fact**: Alcoholic lemonades and colas have an alcohol content comparable to beer or lager.
- **Fact**: Spiking the drinks of others could be fatal; drinking is a factor in half the cases of adult head injury dealt with by hospitals.
- **Fact**: Getting drunk can mean forming an association with someone which you regret; can mean failing to use a condom and can result in a sexually transmitted disease or an unwanted pregnancy.
- **Fact**: Half the **pedestrians** killed in road accidents have more than the drink-driving limit in their bloodstream.
- **Fact**: You can get a criminal record for drunkenness. Being drunk is no excuse for criminal damage or violence.
- **Fact**: Around a thousand under-15s are admitted to hospital every year with alcohol poisoning.
- **Fact**: Alcohol slows reactions and affects skilled activities such as car driving.

**Remember** – The children you teach may be from homes where alcohol is abused.

Having said all that, the use of alcohol – in moderation – can be pleasurable. Many people, especially on the European continent, think that red wine is good for the heart. In these and many other countries, wine is used to accompany and even complement a range of meals!

Alcohol has direct toxic as well as sedative effects on the body and failure to take care of body needs during prolonged periods of excessive drinking may further complicate matters. The effects on major organ systems are cumulative. They include a wide range of digestive system disorders such as ulcers, inflammation of the pancreas and cirrhosis of the liver. The nervous system can be permanently damaged. Blackouts, hallucinations and extreme tremors may occur. These are involved in the most serious alcohol withdrawal syndrome, delirium tremens, which can prove fatal even with prompt treatment. This contrasts with withdrawal from narcotic drugs such as heroin, which rarely results in death. Recent evidence has shown that heavy – and even moderate – drinking during pregnancy can cause serious damage to the unborn child: physical or mental retardation or both.

# Designer drugs – the new dependency

Addiction is a severe form of dependence, usually marked by physical dependence. This state exists when the drug has produced physiological changes in the body with increasing tolerance (increasing amounts of the drug are needed to achieve the same effect) and there are withdrawal symptoms after the drug's effects have worn off. These include nausea, diarrhoea or pain, but vary with the type of drug. Psychological dependence, or habituation, is present when the compulsion to take a drug is strong, even in the absence of physical withdrawal symptoms. In the 1970s, when scientists isolated substances called encephalins, which are naturally occurring opiates in the brain, they discovered what many believe to be the reason behind physical dependence on drugs like opium – the drugs are thought to mimic the action of encephalins. This hypothesis suggests that physical dependence on some drugs may develop in persons who have a lack of these natural substances.

Many children and young people are making an early connection with drugs, often in clubs and social situations. The scene changes so fast that it is impossible to give definitive advice, but examples of the common 'club drugs' are listed in the box below.

In a household survey by the US National Institute on Drug Abuse, more than two-thirds of young adults (aged 18 to 25) reported experience with an illicit substance. Slightly less than 1 in 3 had used marijuana; about 1 in 5 had used hallucinogens; more than 1 in 4 had used cocaine; and more than 1 in 100 had used heroin. Use of heroin tends to be underestimated by household surveys because they don't include, for example, the prison population. Among older adults, more than 1 in 5 reported having used marijuana; more than 1 in 20, hallucinogens; nearly 1 in 10, cocaine; and 1 in 100, heroin. Cocaine use has continued to rise among older adults.

Before teaching young children about drugs, take advice from an expert drugs educator – from the local education authority or from an organisation like the Health Education Authority.

---

**Ecstasy** (E, echoes, XTC, MDMA) – This gives an energy rush and heightened awareness. There is the danger of death from overheating and dehydration.

**Amphetamines** (speed, whiz) – These can contain impurities and lead to dependence.

**Cannabis** (dope, grass, hash, ganga, shit, blow and weed) – This comes from a leafy plant easily cultivated in many countries. It is available as leaf, stalk, seeds (grass) or as a solid brown lump (hash or hashish). It may be smoked with tobacco in a cigarette (joint, reefer or spliff) or taken in a drink or food. Its effects include heightened awareness, raised spirits, increased talk and relaxation. It can also give increased appetite. The downside is that use can lead to paranoia and depression and long-term dependence. There is an increased risk of lung disease from smoking cannabis as against smoking tobacco because cannabis has a high tar factor. Cannabis is a Class B drug – illegal to own, sell or give away.

**Phencyclidine** (PCP, angel dust and rocket fuel) – This became a common drug of abuse in the late 1970s and is a particular menace because it can easily be synthesised. Its effects are quite different from those of other hallucinogens. LSD, for example, produces detachment and euphoria, intensifies vision, and often leads to a crossing of senses (colours are heard, sounds are seen). PCP produces a sense of detachment and a reduction in sensitivity to pain. It may also result in symptoms so like those of acute schizophrenia that even professionals confuse the two states. The combination of this effect and indifference to pain has sometimes resulted in bizarre thinking, occasionally marked by violently destructive behaviour.

**Barbiturates**, cocaine and crack, heroin, LSD, poppers and solvents are other commonly available, addictive drugs.

# Activities

## Level One

Ask the children to make some simple rules for staying healthy in the form of 'dos' and 'don'ts'. How can they stay fit? What actions are likely to make them healthy?

Invite the children to describe the medicines they have taken, and when and how. Ask them to explain why medicines have to be handled with care, and to devise ways of keeping medicines safely. Why are medicine cabinets usually high up on the wall? If a few tablets can do us good, why is it harmful to take a lot more?

Ask children to design a child-proof medicine cupboard.

## Level Two

The children can list ways of keeping healthy such as what to avoid and what to do. Ask them to devise a keep fit plan for a schoolchild. What activities are important, and why? Why are regular visits to the dentist so important? Why does diet matter?

Ask the children to suggest some ways that they can damage their health. What foods and other materials can harm them? How should they protect and take care of their bodies?

Produce a list of positive rules in the form of a 'body handbook'.

## Level Three

Look at the rules for taking medicines. Why are they to be taken in this way? Why could taking them all at once be harmful? Why should they be taken at intervals? Why should you always finish a complete course? Why are medicines locked away and given by adults? Devise some rules for the responsible use of medicines.

Ask the children to link diet and health. Why does a good diet have the effects it does? Why will a poor diet affect them differently?

Challenge stereotypes of health and fitness. We don't all have to be ace sports people. You can be relatively fit when old or disabled. Investigate the paralympics and other events where disability is no bar to fitness.

## Level Four

Look at tobacco smoking. Why do people smoke? What body systems are harmed by smoking? Why is this? Investigate smoking and its effects on the human body. What does it do to you? How can people give up? What can smoking do to the teeth and lungs?

Ask the children to label a picture of the chest and chest organs to show where and how tobacco smoking is harmful.

Be careful not to leave the idea that heavy smokers are all close to death. Many children will know of smokers in their family, and they may become anxious about them. There is evidence that children can encourage relatives to give up, but they should not be unnecessarily upset.

Children could explore the history of smoking – and the other ways that tobacco has been used – chewing tobacco or snuff, for example.

## Level Five

Investigate alcohol and its abuse. Find out what alcohol does to the body systems such as the digestive and circulatory systems.

Why is excess alcohol harmful? Ask the children to explain the effects of alcohol abuse and illustrate them on a body outline.

The children can devise rules for the sensible and moderate use of alcohol by adults. Again, they may be related to someone with alcohol dependence problems, so handle the area with care. Some cultures forbid the use of alcohol, and you should be aware of individual cultural differences.

Investigate drug abuse. Explore the ways that different drugs can affect you, what it means to become addicted and the ways that people try to break addiction. Ask the children to investigate one addictive drug and describe the symptoms and effects to the rest of the class. Choose drugs which the children may be likely to come across. In this, as in all the drug-related activities, involve responsible health professionals.

# Are we all the same?

When you think that we are all made on the same basic body plan, it's amazing how much we all vary. Whether it is height, weight, or our facial features, we are all unique. Even identical twins have their differences.

Environmental (as opposed to genetic) factors – food, exercise, scars and bruises – all add to the differences between the most alike. There are genetic differences as well. There are the long, angular faces and tall bodies of some African tribespeople, such as the Masai, the wide shorter faces and shorter bodies of people from Mongolia, and the squarer faces and in-between height of many Europeans. Then there is also the colour of our skin, from what we call 'white' to what we call 'black' and a multitude of varieties in between!

But, having said we are different – in fact we are all the same! Pigment levels may vary, but skin and hair are very much alike for the whole of the human race.

## Skin – stops our feet fraying

'Why do we have feet?' goes the old joke. 'To stop our legs from fraying at the ends,' is the answer.

Actually, we are all fraying all the time. Our skin is not like a plastic bag, once wrapped round us, never to change. It is a living, growing organ. In fact, it is the largest organ by area and weight in our bodies. It has a surface area of about 1.9 square metres and a weight of 2.7kg. It makes up about 15 per cent of our total body mass. It is equipped with its own blood supply, nerves, sweat glands and follicles from which our hairs grow.

All the time it is losing cells from its surface, only to have new ones grow from below. We replace our skin cells every 19 to 34 days. The lost cells make up a lot of our house dust. On average, we have a completely new skin every 27 days. The top layer of our skin – the epidermis – varies in thickness. It is thinnest on our eyelids – and thickest on our palms and soles.

So, regardless of its colour, our skin has a number of important functions besides stopping all our inside bits falling out.

## Fascinating facts

● Even identical twins have tiny differences in their fingerprints. Sir Francis Galton first classified fingerprints in 1892. In 1901, Sir Edward Henry established the first Fingerprint Branch at Scotland Yard.

## No sweat?

We need to keep a constant body temperature (see Chapter 6). But there are times when we may overheat – in a hot climate, in warm clothes or when we have a fever. How are we to lose that excess heat? It would be handy if someone could come along and give us a mild spray with cooling water. The water would evaporate, and it would take our body heat with it. We get the same sort of sensation when we put some liquids on our skin – aftershave, witch-hazel. They evaporate and our skin feels cool.

Fortunately, our skin is equipped to self-cool. Tubes called sweat glands pour out liquid onto our skin, and as this liquid evaporates away, the heat is taken with it. The sweat from these tiny coiled tubes has salt in it, which is why you need to eat salt with your food in a hot climate. On average, we lose half a litre of water a day. Sweat itself has no smell but it is an ideal food for skin bacteria which do smell.

There are about three million sweat glands all over your body, with large numbers on your palms and soles. Antiperspirants help to slow sweating. Other products absorb the sweat without blocking the pores, allowing the water to evaporate slowly. Deodorants mask odours and sometimes contain anti-bacterial chemicals, too.

## First line of defence

Our skin is also an excellent protection against infection. It stops harmful bacteria entering our bodies – protecting us against many diseases. If we cut our skin, the blood clots to stop further bleeding.

The tiny platelets floating in your blood rush to plug the gap. They become sticky, gluing themselves to the blood vessel wall. Then they send chemical messengers into the blood. These cries for help make the blood form a net of threads which trap blood cells forming a jelly which quickly hardens into a scab.

## Gentle touch

Our skin is also an excellent sense organ, telling us about the world around us. In it there are sensors for pressure, heat, touch and pain and together they give us a clear idea of what we are touching. Bits of us – our fingertips and tongues, for example – are more sensitive than others, such as our backs or feet. We are more likely to be handling things with our fingers than our backs.

These sensitive areas have many more sensors than our backs and feet. You can tell the difference between two needle points a tiny distance apart on your fingertip but they feel like just one on your back.

## It is waterproof

It's not just that we can go out in the rain. The skin holds in the fluid that bathes our cells and prevents us from drying out. A waxy material called sebum from the skin's sebaceous glands keeps it slightly greasy, making it waterproof too. We may have problems with sebum at puberty, though, when we produce rather too much of the stuff, leading to blocked pores and acne. If bacteria build up behind the sebum, a pore can become infected and inflamed as a spot.

## It resists wear and tear

We may lose skin cells every time we have a vigorous rub with a towel, but our skin is remarkably long-lasting. It is estimated that, if our skin were made from stainless steel, it would wear out in seven years.

### It comes in a range of attractive colours

The colour of your skin depends upon the amount of a pigment called melanin there is in it. This brown colouring is most concentrated in darker skins but many white people produce more melanin after some days in the sun, making a protective suntan. The melanin helps to protect the skin from harmful ultraviolet rays and so helps to avoid sunburn.

### It can burn

Sunlight is good for you, causing your skin to produce vitamin D and making you feel healthy. But too much sun can lead to sunburn and sunstroke, or even to cell damage and skin cancers. Sunscreens can help protect your skin; they have an SPF – a sun protection factor. White people's skin and sensitive skins need an SPF of 15+, while skin that tans easily may need an SPF of only 8–10. Oils, milks, creams, sprays and gels all contain sun filters although oils are less likely to contain much.

### It needs to be kept clean

You can keep this wonderful organ clean in three different ways. Soaps or detergents help the oily dirt wash off in water. Creams of different kinds actually dissolve the dirt, and so does the alcohol in a cleansing lotion. Scrubbing with a brush, flannel or sponge helps take the oily skin debris away.

### Sadly, it gets old

As we age, our skin tends to get rougher and drier. It becomes more deeply lined. It can become streaky and blotchy in colour, and it becomes less elastic. The protein fibres in our skin lose their spring. You can see this if you pinch the skins of an old and a young person. The older skin takes far longer to return to shape. Skin ages faster if it is exposed to a lot of sunshine.

Skin creams and lotions can prevent drying out or even put water back into the skin, softening it and helping it retain its elasticity. Moisturising creams are made from oils and water. The water evaporates from the skin, leaving the oil on the surface.

## Nails are skin, too

Nails are made from keratin, a tough protein which is also the main constituent of skin and hair. Nails grow from a nail-bed just above your last toe or finger joint. Their job is to protect your delicate finger and toe ends. Illness, or too much washing (doctors suffer from it!), can leave white marks in your nails which take some time to grow out.

Fingernails grow at around 2cm a year. The longer the finger, the faster the nail growth. So the middle finger grows the fastest. Fingernails grow four times as fast as toenails.

## Fascinating facts

- Goose bumps or goose-pimples are caused by the contraction of muscles in your skin. This is a kind of activity and all activities produce heat. So it is a useful body reaction when we are cold.

- Tattoos can be removed by several techniques, including grafting and scrubbing salt into the skin. Some solutions can break up the tattoo pigments but they produce scars.

## Hair

We have around 100,000 hairs on our heads. Blonds have the most, with as many as 140,000, and redheads the fewest, with about 90,000. Brunette numbers are between these two. You lose between 100 and 150 hairs every day, but these usually grow back. Hair grows from tubes or follicles. As new cells are formed in the follicle, they push the old ones ahead of them and they are forced out as hairs.

Human hair grows 12cm a year. It grows faster in the summer because the warm weather increases the blood flow to the scalp. A hair lasts for between two and six years before falling out. The average scalp produces between one and one and a half kilometres of hair each month.

## It's in the genes

Family background determines many of our characteristics. We inherit from both our parents but we may also reflect characteristics of previous generations. Some inherited characteristics are dominant – brown eyes over blue, for example – but blue eyes keep recurring in later generations, nevertheless.

**Warning** – be careful not to cause distress when talking about inheritance information. Some children were once told that brown-eyed parents cannot have blue-eyed children. This caused great pain and was incorrect!

Some babies are born bald; others with thick hair on their heads. All the hair follicles you will ever have are formed in your first 12–16 weeks in your mother's womb. Baby hair usually falls out, to be replaced by hair in the colour the child will usually have for life. Bald babies quickly grow hair, too.

Some people – especially men – become bald as they grow older. This tends to run in families. Their head is not completely hairless – it is covered in tiny, fine hairs. Hair cracks as we get older, and these tiny cracks have air bubbles in them which reflect the light, making hair silvery or grey. (You see the same effect in the bark of silver birches.) The finer hair of youth may thicken in middle age, becoming finer as you grow older.

## Fascinating facts

- Straight hair is round in cross-section; wavy hair is oval; curly hair is flat.

- Hair and nails do not grow after death. It is the drying and shrinking of the body that creates this illusion.

- A monk living in Madras had the longest recorded hair at 7.93m long.

- A thousand hairs are strong enough to support an adult.

- Dandruff is made from clumps of skin cells stuck together with oily sebum. Dandruff is common in greasy hair, and regular washing should clear it.

- Men develop beard hair at puberty, which is thicker than scalp hair and grows about a centimetre a month. Men spend, on average, 100 days shaving in their lifetimes.

# Activities

## Level One

Ask the children to name the main parts of their bodies and to label them on a picture. Use simple differences to group the children in different ways, for example by height, hand or foot size. Produce simple graphical representations of the children, perhaps using ICT.

Ensure that everyone is fairly represented – so that the tall are not seen as in some way 'better' than the smaller. You could conduct an activity where everyone tries to curl up inside hoops on the ground. Smaller children will be able to fit inside smaller hoops. Emphasise that bodies change with age and that small children may not be small adults.

## Level Two

Ask the children to make comparisons between themselves and others, looking at differences and (more difficult) similarities. They can draw themselves and a friend and annotate the similarities and differences.

They can produce simple block graphs, such as 'hair colours in our class' and 'eye colours in my group'. Be careful to avoid racial or other stereotypes.

Look for similarities between the children, for example what we all need to survive and how we are alike. Invite the children to make their own groupings. Record the groupings as diagrams and graphs. Overlapping Venn diagrams can represent two or more overlapping groups.

## Level Three

Ask the children to record changes in themselves as they have grown and then changes they expect to follow. They can draw themselves at different ages and stages. They could order photographs of themselves and record what they can and can't do, and could and couldn't do in the past.

Investigate reasons for the similarities and differences between people; these may include diet, upbringing and family background. Be aware of family differences such as adoption, and remember that children do not always present their parents' characteristics.

## Level Four

Ask the children to record and explain the purpose of the smaller parts of their bodies, such as ear lobes, Achilles' tendons and nails. How do these differ between the children? Who has small ear lobes or thicker eyebrows?

Tell the children to record their understanding of their skin and hair. They should list the ways of keeping their hair and skin healthy and in good condition. Investigate skin and hair as a body organ/system.

Make some basic hygiene rules. Is excessive cleanliness a good thing? Challenge obsessive concerns that are encouraged in the media. Be aware of family backgrounds that make personal hygiene difficult.

## Level Five

Explore individual differences and body symmetry. Use a mirror held vertically on a full-face picture to show that the face is not symmetrical. Explore differences between left- and right-handed skills.

The children can produce simple diagrams of the skin and how hairs grow. They could explain how sweat cools the skin and a covering of hair can reduce heat loss and keep you warm.

Ask the children to explore the range of hair colours in the class, and compare this with the range in the school. Ask them to record differences in body temperature with exercise, and the physiological results of sweating. Use a safe liquid that evaporates quickly, like tincture of iodine, to explore how evaporation can lower temperature.

Explore the range of differences between people and relate these to their background, climate and way of life. Look, for example, at how people from hot countries are frequently tall and thin, offering a large body area for the loss of heat; while those from cold countries may be stocky to retain heat.

Celebrate human differences and range in a picture display, a book or drama.